Finance Capital and
Uneven Development

Finance Capital and Uneven Development

Gary P. Green

Westview Press / Boulder and London

Westview Special Studies in Social, Political, and Economic Development

Copyright © 1987 by Westview Press, Inc.

Published in 1987 in the United States of America by Westview Press, Inc.; Frederick
A. Praeger, Publisher; 5500 Central Avenue, Boulder, Colorado 80301

Library of Congress Cataloging-in-Publication Data
Green, Gary P.
Finance capital and uneven development/by Gary P. Green.
   p. cm.--(Westview special studies in social, political, and
economic development)
   ISBN 0-8133-7420-0
   1. Financial institutions--United States. 2. Credit--United
States. 3. Agricultural credit--United States. 4. Southern States-
-Economic conditions--Regional disparities. 5. Debts, External-
-Developing countries. I. Title. II. Series.
HG181.G72 1987
332.7'0973--dc19
                                                       87-22945
                                                            CIP

Printed and bound in the United States of America

The paper used in this publication meets the requirements
of the American National Standard for Permanence of Paper
for Printed Library Materials Z39.48-1984.

6   5   4   3   2   1

Contents

Tables

Acknowledgments

Many people have contributed to the completion of this manuscript. Much of the theoretical material in this book was developed in my doctoral dissertation on rural banks and the changing structure of agriculture. I want to thank Bill Heffernan for providing a stimulating environment for my graduate work at the University of Missouri.

The staff at the Institute of Community and Area Development (ICAD) at the University of Georgia were instrumental in the production of the manuscript. In particular, Linda Edwards conscientiously typed countless drafts for me. Lynn Igoe, at the University of North Carolina, carefully edited the manuscript and made many useful suggestions.

I want to thank my colleagues in the Sociology Department at the University of Georgia. They have provided an excellent intellectual environment and social support for my work. Phil McMichael read the entire manuscript and made many useful suggestions. Cindy Holiny, Hea-in Choi, and Farshad Araghi provided research assistance for several of the chapters.

I know that the manuscript could not have been completed without the help of Leann Tigges. I can never properly express my appreciation for Leann's support and encouragement. Leann carefully read the manuscript and helped me work through many of the ideas in the book. She has been a most loyal supporter.

Gary P. Green

1

Towards a Political Economy of Credit

Uneven development is a prominent feature of advanced capitalism, characterized by rapid growth in some sectors and regions and decline in others. In the United States, loss of jobs in the auto and steel industries and growth in other industries, particularly in the service sector, have been well documented (Bluestone and Harrison, 1982). The rise of the "New South" and deindustrialization in the "Rust Belt" are examples of this process working on a regional level. Finally, the growing disparity in growth rates between advanced and less developed societies is an example of uneven development occurring on a global level.

Among social scientists are many disputes over the causes and consequences of uneven development. Neoclassical economists and modernization theorists argue that differences in the rate of development are caused by factors influencing the efficiency of production and distribution (e.g., productivity, access to resources, proximity to markets). These theorists assume that the benefits of industrialization will eventually reach all groups, regions, and sectors. Technological advancements are a key to reducing differences in productivity, the demand for raw materials, and the importance of proximity to markets. Therefore, social and economic factors prohibiting technological change (e.g., traditional values and institutions) must be changed to spur development. Development leads to greater specialization of tasks and an increased division of labor. Consequently, unfettered capitalism eliminates significant differences in the rate of development between economic sectors and regions. Some level of unevenness, however, is desirable if capitalism is to work efficiently.

Keynesian economists and liberal social theorists argue that institutional barriers in capitalism prevent lagging regions, industries, and nations from catching-up with developed sectors. Often this relationship between developed and underdeveloped sectors is characterized by these theorists as dependent or exploitative. Through a process of unequal exchange, the dominant sector prospers at the expense of other sectors. Technological development, according to these theorists, exacerbates the tendencies toward uneven development in capitalism by increasing the mobility of capital. In addition, unequal access to information and to credit becomes more critical in determining the rate of development when new technology is introduced. According to Keynesian economists, capitalism is basically sound, but it requires some adjustments. Uneven rates of development can be reduced by state action or institutional change not requiring a restructuring of the entire economic system. The theorists often identify the state as a key factor in either facilitating or retarding development. A strong state will promote the types of changes necessary for development to occur.

Radical political economists and Marxists take a much different stance toward analyzing uneven development. These theorists argue that uneven development is a product of historical forces, such as class conflict (Fox, 1978) or political conflict (Markusen, 1979; 1980). Uneven development is a consequence of obstacles capitalists encounter in their drive to expand. These obstacles may be related to problems associated with production relations or circulation. These problems develop for several reasons: overproduction or underconsumption, rising wages, or technological advances. Different historical conditions have required different strategies by the capitalist class. According to Marx, there is a tendency for capitalism to produce a growing disparity in the rates of development among sectors and regions. This position differs with the neoclassical position by focusing on the social and historical context in which development occurs. In other words, these social and historical dimensions influence the character and extent of development. In addition, technology and state policy reflect the class character of capitalism. Thus, technological change tends to exacerbate uneven development in capitalism; and uneven development is facilitated by state policy promoting the conditions for technological change. For radical theorists, the key to eliminating uneven development is abolishing the class character of capitalism.

In this analysis, I adopt the radical position by demonstrating how finance capital contributes to uneven development among economic sectors, regions, and nations. The structure of finance capital distributes capital inefficiently and inequitably. In addition, the relationship between finance capital and the state limits the possibilities of political action to alleviate the problems of uneven development caused by finance capital. Although the analysis is largely structural, I believe a radical analysis of development can incorporate the role of subjects.

CREDIT AND ITS ROLE IN DEVELOPMENT

Almost all social scientists agree that the banking system is instrumental in facilitating economic growth and development. Gerschenkron (1962) asserts that the banking system has been a prime source of capital and entrepreneurship in advanced industrialized societies. Neoclassical and Keynesian economists, however, consider financial institutions to be passive, simply responding to demand (Gurley and Shaw, 1955). Bankers are conceptualized as perfectly rational actors responding to differing economic opportunities. In making their decisions where to invest limited resources, bankers have perfect information available to them and are able to assess the risk and profitability of various types of loans and investments.[1] By lending capital to firms, industries, and regions considered most profitable, bankers ensure that the market operates in an efficient and equitable manner.

Although there is theoretical support for emphasizing the role of credit in economic development, empirical studies show at best a weak relationship between the performance of commercial banks and economic growth. Milkhove and Weisblat's (1982) investigation of the effects of rural bank performance on economic growth reveals only an extremely weak relationship. Dreese (1974), in a study of credit and employment growth, concludes that employment growth is a better predictor of loan growth than the reverse. Verbrugge summarizes the literature on rural banking:

> Despite the problems with the banking system in rural areas and with the various credit programs outlined, the fact remains that while financing is an important aspect of development, it is not the primary determinant. The more fundamental characteristics of an area such as market access, transportation facilities, labor supply, and resources are the causal forces in development. If a project or a new plant is projected to be a profitable venture, funding will be available from one of several sources described above or from the national money and capital markets. There is virtually no evidence to support a position that lack of financing has impeded the development of an area (1975:36-37).

An alternative view of this relationship between credit and development is Marx's theory of finance capital. According to Marx, the credit system actively promotes uneven development and economic crises among industries, regions, and nations. In its role as an intermediary between savers and borrowers, the financial system becomes a social clearinghouse for capital, expanding and channeling capital's accumulation through its unique ability to create money capital. As the financial system collects money income, it distributes money capital inequitably among various industries, regions, and nations. According to this view, bankers consider noneconomic factors in their lending decisions. Bankers are not perfectly rational, but tend to maximize security and reduce their risk in the loan portfolio. As a result, bankers may not lend to various sectors, regions, or firms because these loans would be too risky, even though they may be profitable and contribute to the growth and development of the economy. Because credit becomes a commodity in capitalist societies, allocation decisions for credit are based on exchange value rather than use value. This has implications for the relationship between credit and development. In addition, the organizational structure of financial markets influences the allocation of capital; increased concentration exacerbates the tendency for uneven development. Reduced competition in the banking industry influences the process by which capital is allocated. A more centralized credit system will tend to be more risk aversive.

Theorists adopting this latter position assume that financial institutions are active, rather than passive,

actors promoting economic development. Through its role
as a social clearinghouse for capital, the financial
system defines the parameters for capital investment.
The financial system is creating and defining the
character of economic development. That is, a capitalist
financial system allocates capital on the basis of profit
maximization and makes assessments on risks involved in
investments. This risk assessment is a social, not an
individual decision. By social, I mean that allocation
decisions are imposed on finance capitalists through
competition and that these decisions have social
consequences, influencing the rate and character of
development. Financial markets are not things, but are
socially constructed and reproduced. As a result, the
social structure influences how the market distributes
capital to various sectors and regions.

Following Minsky (1978), I argue that financial
systems tend to produce economic instability and crises.
Expansion of credit fuels overspeculation, which
contributes to the boom and bust cycles in capitalism.
Although the expansion of credit is an important
ingredient in the process of economic development, it
does not ensure that development will occur. In fact,
the rapid expansion of credit in the United States in the
1970s has produced increased instability in the economy.
In response to economic crises, the state must intervene
increasingly by making available public sources of
credit, regulating financial institutions, and
guaranteeing financial commitments through its role as
lender-of-last-resort. Influence over capital flows
becomes an important tool for the state to direct
economic development and growth.

In this view of the role of credit in development,
financial institutions occupy a pivotal position in the
capital accumulation process. This view does not mean
that finance capital is the only cause of uneven
development. Instead, the underlying factors of uneven
development are the nature of class struggle, the
strength of the capitalist state, and market forces in
the world economy. In a sense, the financial system is
not independent of the capitalist economy, but reflects
and reproduces capitalist social relations. It is the
social character of credit systems that makes it
difficult for lagging regions, sectors, and industries to
improve their position relative to leading regions,
sectors, and industries.

This argument does not rest on identifying motives

and intentions of finance capitalists. Actions of
finance capitalists frequently have unintended
consequences. I am concerned primarily with the
consequences of the behavior of finance capitalists and
the structure in which their activity is located. Hence,
my evidence will be based primarily on who benefits from
using credit and the distributional consequences of
credit. It is possible to discern the influence of
finance capitalists on capital flows by examining
differential access to credit. My assumption is that
social organization will influence how financial markets
function.

OUTLINE OF BOOK

In this book, I extend previous research on finance
capital theoretically and methodologically. Most
researchers examining finance capital focus on its
relationship to other segments of capital (landed and
industrial). Many of these analyses are static,
neglecting the impact of finance capital on the
accumulation process, and industrial and political
change. I argue that finance capital is an agent of
social transformation. Financial institutions play an
important role as mediator between savers and borrowers.
As they play this role, financial institutions establish
the rate and direction of capital flows. This
conceptualization of financial institutions, as actively
producing industrial change and development, radically
differs from that in the literature on credit and
development.

Second, this analysis makes an important contribution
to recent policy discussions concerning growing and
declining industries and regions. The strength of
finance capital influences the state's organizational
capacity to solve these economic problems. The
structural separation of financial institutions from
commerce prevents the state from readily using the
financial system as a tool to promote industrial and
technological change. Political solutions ignoring the
role of capital flows in development will only be
treating the symptoms of the problem. In addition, the
growing transnational character of finance capital makes
it much more difficult for the state to influence capital
flows directly.

I believe my analysis also makes an important

methodological contribution to the literature on finance
capital. My approach is to examine these theoretical
issues by developing a comparative analysis of capital
flows at three levels: industry, region, and nation-
state. This method permits a comparative examination of
patterns in the way finance capital affects economic
development and in the state's relationship to financial
markets.

In chapter 2, I integrate the literature on corporate
control with the literature on credit and economic
development. I develop a model of the impact of
corporate control on the type and rate of development.
This model suggests that the development of finance
capital undermines the competitive basis of financial
markets. Organizational changes in financial markets
contribute to increased concentration and centralization
of market economies. The expansion of credit brings
about change in the rate of development within economic
sectors, regions, and nations. The conservative
character of financial institutions tends to allocate
capital inefficiently and inequitably.

A second proposition drawn from my theoretical model
and developed in chapter 3 is that there is a dialectical
relationship between the state and the financial system.
The financial system influences the type and extent of
state involvement in market economies. Control over
capital flows has become increasingly important in the
state's effort to promote economic development. As
Zysman (1983) indicates, the strength of finance capital
affects the state's influence over capital flows. A more
centralized financial system lets the state more
directly influence decisions regarding the allocation of
money capital. Changes in the organizational structure
of credit markets threaten to exacerbate the
contradictions of market economies. On the other hand,
the state defines the character of finance capital and
the organizational structure of capital markets.

The next three chapters are case studies assessing
the theoretical model. In chapter 4 I provide an
analysis of the U.S. farm financial crisis. This crisis
can be traced to the boom in agriculture during the
1970s, when the demand for agricultural commodities was
extremely strong, the value of land increased
dramatically, and farmers were encouraged to borrow as
much debt capital as possible to expand their operations.
State policy reduced the risk involved in production and
promoted capital investment in agriculture. These

conditions made agriculture an extremely good investment
during this period and fueled the growth and expansion of
capital. The 1980s, however, are characterized by
extremely low commodity prices, declining land values,
and farm foreclosures. I present evidence suggesting
that the farm financial crisis not only will lead to
fewer and larger farms, but also may bring about a change
in the ownership and control of farmland.

In the second case study, I assess the development of
the New South. Historically, the South has been an
underdeveloped region lacking capital. In this chapter,
I examine competing explanations for the South's
underdevelopment and for the lack of capital development
in the region. The rise of the New South, and the role
of finance capital in its development provide an
interesting case study of the effects of finance capital
on regional development. This development is somewhat
precarious, depending largely on the outcome of the
conflict between regional and national finance
capitalists. In addition, this development has been
uneven within the region, particularly between urban and
rural areas. A major factor influencing regional flows
of capital is deregulation of financial institutions.

Chapter 6 is an examination of the Third World debt
crisis. Commercial lending to Third World countries
increased dramatically in the 1970s as U.S. and European
banks were flooded with capital from OPEC countries.
After the surge of capital into Third World countries,
the world economy slid into a recession. To meet their
interest payments, Third World countries have been forced
to borrow more from commercial banks, leading to
pyramiding of credit. This crisis is not simply a result
of the recession in the early 1980s, but is a consequence
of the type of credit advanced and the structural
position of Third World countries in the world market. I
examine proposals for alleviating the world debt crisis.
If the problem is viewed as a liquidity crisis, it is
assumed that lower interest rates, higher growth rates in
the developing countries, and additional capital
(primarily from public sources) will alleviate the
crisis. If the problem is defined as a solvency crisis,
however, structural changes in the Third World, and their
relationship to developed countries, are required.
The transnational character of capital makes in
increasingly difficult for individual states to influence
the direction of capital flows in the world market.

In the concluding chapter, I examine the consequences

of these findings for policy and development strategies.
Credit is commonly seen as a panacea for economic
problems in industries, regions, and developing nations.
My analysis suggests that credit is double-edged,
producing some benefits, but also contributing to new
structural problems. Many of the problems are associated
with the structure of financial institutions. I argue
that alternative credit institutions must be developed to
aid lagging industries, regions, and nations. These
alternatives, however, are limited in their ability to
alleviate development problems. The credit system is
embedded in class relations and reflects the class
character of capitalism.

NOTES

1. There is no consensus in the literature as to
whether bankers emphasize risk or profits most in their
loan evaluations. In most cases, there are significant
differences between the two criteria.

2

Corporate Control and Economic Development

Marx's theory of finance capital has received little attention among social theorists. The theory of finance capital was central to the writings of early 20th-century Marxists, such as Hilferding ([1910] 1981) and Lenin (1917). These theorists identified a new stage of capitalism marked by the ascendancy of finance capital.[1] Marx argued that over the course of capitalist development, three species of capitalists emerged: industrial, finance (money), and landowning capitalists.[2] All share three forms of surplus value: profit, interest, and rent. The development of finance capitalists and landowning capitalists, however, presupposes the existence of industrial capital (Balinsky, 1970).

These early theorists reasoned that development of the joint-stock company made industrial capitalists increasingly dependent on financial capital because of the enlarged capital requirements of this form of economic organization. Industrial capitalists' dependency on external sources of capital undermines their control and influence over the firm. The rise of finance capital produces additional structural contradictions exacerbating the tendency towards crisis. For example, finance capital imposes increased rationality on markets, but also pressures capitalists to maximize short-term interests.

According to Marx ([1894] 1981), the credit system has a dual or contradictory character. On one hand, it lays the conditions for and speeds the development of capitalist accumulation. For example, the credit system counteracts the tendency for the average rate of profit to fall by enlarging the scope and tempo of capital accumulation in the productive sphere and accelerating the concentration of capital. By speeding the turnover rate of capital, the credit system overcomes many of the obstacles to capitalist development (e.g., underconsumption, rising organic composition of capital). On the other hand, the credit system is the principle lever of overproduction and excessive speculation. Through its unique ability to create money capital, the credit system promotes indebtedness and makes it increasingly problematic for the state to stabilize the economy.

Therefore, Marx's analysis of credit involves an examination of the relationship between finance and industrial capitalists and its consequences for the accumulation process. For Marx, money capital plays a pivotal role in the accumulation process:

> The credit system hence accelerates the material development of the productive forces and the creation of the world market, which it is the historical task of the capitalist mode of production to bring to a certain level of development, as material foundations for the new form of production. At the same time, credit accelerates the violent outbreaks of this contradiction, crises, and with these the elements of dissolution of the old mode of production ([1894] 1981:572).

In this chapter, I review sociological debates concerning the nature of corporate control and the performance of large capitalist firms. I discuss the structural relationships between the firm and managers, stockholders, and financial institutions, and how these relationships influence corporate performance. The rise of finance capital redefines relationships among various segments of the capitalist class and has important implications for the accumulation process. Second, I develop a structural analysis of credit in advanced capitalist societies, focusing on the functions and consequences of capitalist credit systems. The credit system actively promotes uneven development and economic crises among industries, regions, and nations. Through their control over capital flows, finance capitalists allocate credit in an inequitable manner and encourage overspeculation and overproduction. These two issues, corporate control and the role of finance capital in the accumulation process, must be treated as two highly interrelated features of Marx's theory of finance capital.

THEORIES OF CORPORATE CONTROL

The Managerial Revolution Thesis

For several decades, the thesis that ownership and control have been severed in the largest corporations of capitalist societies was accepted as "fact" by social scientists. This thesis has been advanced by conservatives, liberals, even radicals. This alleged separation in ownership and control is considered to be a consequence of the increased scale of production. One version of this argument, the managerial revolution thesis, states that technological developments have increased rapidly the scale of production, and consequently enlarged the capital requirements for production. Increased capital requirements make it practically impossible for a small group of families or individuals to exercise control over corporate activities and decision making. As a result, control in the largest corporations has shifted from the propertied class to managerial and technical personnel (Berle and Means, 1932; Burnham, 1941). For many social theorists, this historical shift in control is an indicator of the destruction of the old class structure and political economy of capitalism (Bell, 1958; Dahrendorf, 1959; Parsons, 1953, Sorokin, 1953).

One consequence of the separation of ownership and control, according to these theorists, is a change in the stratification system from a class to an occupationally-based system. Occupational attainment is based allegedly on individual achievement rather than social class advantages. This reasoning is consistent with the functionalist school of inequality, which argues that if inequality persists in modern society it is based on skill and ability rather than on ownership of property and wealth (Davis and Moore, 1945).

The shift to managerial control not only transforms the relationship between property and power, but also the performance of capitalist firms. Managers of large corporations maximize goals other than profit, such as growth and security, which often conflict with the immediate economic interests of stockholders (Simon,

1956). According to managerialists, promotion and tenure
for corporate managers is based on the steady growth of
the firm. The costs of taking risk and maximizing
profits tend to exceed the benefits of these activities.
Berle and Means' (1932) study of large corporations in
the United States was the first to suggest that the
growth of the modern corporation would produce a
qualitative change in the performance of management.
Structural changes in corporations would pressure
management to ultimately be more concerned about the
social consequences of their action.

> The owners of passive property, by surrendering
> control and responsibility over the active property,
> have surrendered the right that the corporation
> should be operated in their sole interest; they have
> released the community from the obligation to
> protect them to the full extent implied in the
> doctrine of strict property rights. At the same
> time, the controlling groups, by means of the
> extension of corporate powers, have in their own
> interest broken the bars of tradition which require
> that the corporation be operated solely for the
> benefit of the owners of passive property. (Berle and
> Means, 1932:311-12).

Berle and Means envision the modern corporation as a
vehicle for societal improvement. The increased size of
capitalist firms enables managers to meet their capital
requirements from retained earnings, thereby reducing
their dependency on financial institutions. Increased
firm size, therefore, reduces the influence of
stockholders and other corporate actors (finance
capitalists). The result is corporations controlled by
managers performing in a manner consistent with the
interests of the public rather than stockholders. Berle
and Means present evidence suggesting that this
transition already had taken place by the 1930s. The
result was a corporate system driven by public rather
than private needs.

Criticism of the Managerial Revolution Thesis. A
frequent criticism of Berle and Means' classic study is
that they chose an arbitrary level of stock ownership to
define management control. Eisenbeis and McCall (1972)
conclude that corporate control could be achieved with a
relatively small concentration of stock. Effective
control can be assured with as little as a 5 percent

holding in many cases. Goldsmith and Parmelee (1940), using data Congress collected on the 20 largest stockholders of the 200 largest nonfinancial corporations, find 46 percent of the firms to be owner controlled. Later, Villarejo (1961) discovers that more than 60 percent of the 250 largest U.S. corporations were controlled by a community of interest based on stock ownership. Finally, Lundberg (1969) indicates that 60 percent of the 200 largest firms were characterized as owner controlled in the mid 1960s.

The managerial revolution thesis was attacked not only on empirical grounds, but also on theory. Zeitlin (1974) criticizes this research for its method and measurement and its problematic conceptualization of control.

> Our review of discrepant findings on the alleged separation of ownership and control in the large corporations in the United States, and of the problems entailed in obtaining reliable and valid evidence on the actual ownership interests involved in a given corporation, should make it clear that the absence of control by proprietary interests in the largest corporations is by no means an "unquestionable," "incontrovertible," "singular," or "critical" social "fact" (p. 1107).

Zeitlin argues that an absence of a certain level of stock is not sufficient evidence to accept or reject the managerial revolution thesis. For Zeitlin, control is much more problematic than the managerialists have assumed in their research. Direct control may be fairly uncommon and structural constraints on managerial decision making may be a much more prevalent form of control. Zeitlin's approach toward understanding control is the focus of the class cohesion, bank control, and bank hegemony theories.

Class Cohesion Theory

Class cohesion theorists argue that managers in the largest corporations are not autonomous, but are constrained to maximize profits. These theorists point to a set of institutional constellations structuring the profit imperative in a capitalist society (Scott, 1979).[3] Outside control exists in a variety of forms, such as intercorporate stockholding and interlocking directorates, and provides cohesion within the capitalist class (Allen, 1978; Mariolis, 1977; Mintz and Schwartz, 1977). Cliques of corporations are connected through interlocking directorates forming a controlling interest in several different corporations. These relationships within the capitalist class provide a means for developing a common set of goals and world view. Although the effect of these interest groups on management-controlled firms has not been examined empirically, it has been hypothesized that they intensify profit discipline.

A major criticism of the managerialists' prediction that management-controlled firms would perform differently from owner-controlled firms has been that managers are often from the same social class as owners, and in many cases, are substantial investors in the firm. Similar social backgrounds and social ties often yield the same orientations toward business, and the economy in general (Domhoff, 1983; Mills, 1956; Mizruchi, 1982). Even when top level managers do not come from the owners' social class, a form of social selectivity operates which promotes individuals who develop the same interpretation of social reality as owners. This selectivity operates in the process of hiring and promoting top level managers; it produces "like minds" in the most powerful corporate positions. Of critical importance is the grooming of a "business ethic," which guarantees that profits are the most important consideration in corporate decision making. Top level managers also frequently own voting stock, producing interests that are remarkably similar to those of the majority stockholders in the corporation. Many large corporations maintain stock option or profit-sharing plans that tie much of the manager's current and future income to firm profits.

A number of positive and negative incentives are built into the structure of the large corporation and its environment to encourage managers of management-controlled firms to be as concerned as the stockholders about the firm's profit rate. The salaries of top level management in the largest corporations are strongly correlated to profit rates of the firm (Larner, 1970; Masson, 1971). Negative incentives, such as dismissal, are also positively correlated to the profit rate of the firm. James and Soref (1981) demonstrate that the profit rate is strongly related to executive firing, a relationship that holds up for both owner- and management-controlled firms.

Factors other than direct ownership and compensation fix managerial boundaries and press managers toward the pursuit of owner-consistent objectives. Several market penalties exist for companies that perform poorly, such as low credit ratings and stock prices. A poor credit rating or a drop in the company's stock prices may lead to a loss of managerial autonomy and discretion. Survival of the firm is based largely on its ability to obtain credit, which is indirectly based on its profit rate. Without a good credit rating or an improvement in the price of the company's stock, it is difficult for managers to maintain stockholders' support. As long as managers produce a reasonable rate of return, in the eyes of stockholders and bankers, they are likely to retain their "autonomy." Threat of corporate takeover also influences performance of the firm. Undervalued firms tend to be taken over more frequently than overvalued firms (Herman, 1981). Takeover bids are often initiated by depressed stock prices and result in outsiders directly appealing to stockholders, thereby circumventing managers entirely and reducing their autonomy.

An often overlooked factor motivating managers is the profit-oriented value system existing within the business world.

> [The] power of ownership is such that the application of criteria other than profit as a basis of systematic valuation has been ruled off the agenda. The profit-oriented value system may have greater applicability to nonowners as managers than to owner/managers, since there is considerable uncertainty about the institutional role of the manager, and there will be a greater tendency for him--than, say, for the professional--to concentrate on pecuniary gain; i.e., to concentrate on that aspect of self-interest which has least dependence upon meeting expectations implicit in a normative code (Herman, 1981:102).

The proposition that profit considerations are embedded in the ideology, rules, and norms of the corporation has been criticized by others who argue that managers are not motivated exclusively by economic considerations (Simon, 1956). Guided by "satisficing" rather than profit-maximizing principles, managers use the market power of the large corporation to minimize

uncertainty and unreliability of markets, and maximize
technical efficiency and effective planning, not profits.
To test the proposition about the profit motive of
mangers, a plethora of studies have contrasted and
compared the profit rates of management- and owner-
controlled firms.   Most of these studies have found
statistical differences between the profit ratios of two
kinds of firms (Elliot, 1972; Kamerschen, 1968; Zeitlin
and Norich, 1979).   Herman (1981:260) indicates that "in
an important sense, the success of large corporations
follows in part from their being designed to be less
socially responsible than smaller local enterprises."
Several studies compare types of firms on measures of
social responsibility.   These studies examine corporate
charitable contributions (Baumol et al., 1970),
relocation decisions (Bluestone and Harrison, 1980),
environmental standards (Nader, 1964), occupational
health and consumer health and safety (Brodeur, 1974).
The data overwhelmingly suggest that large corporations
are less socially responsible than small enterprises.
When management- and owner-controlled firms are compared,
there are few differences with regard to social
responsibility.
     Even if control of large corporations has shifted
from owners to managers, these studies suggest that it
has not had any consequences for the performance of
firms. Managers make decisions that are generally in the
best interests of stockholders.   Incentives and penalties
encourage managers to maximize profits.   In addition, the
capitalist class is able to structure much managerial
decision making by restricting the range of options
available to managers.
     Criticism of the Class Cohesion Position.   The class
cohesion position, however, suffers from two major
weaknesses. First, theorists must rely on a subjectivist
account of ruling class control.   For members of the
ruling class to maintain control, they must occupy the
most important positions and generally impose their will
on managers.   In this sense, class cohesion theory has
frequently been criticized for being individualistic,
ignoring other forms of structural control.
     Second, class cohesion theorists play down the
complex of corporate relations that exist in capitalist
economies. Recent analyses, such as Burt's (1983),
indicate that patterns of buying and selling among
sectors of the economy constrain the firm's ability to
make profits. These intercorporate relations may have a

greater impact on the performance of capitalist firms than does their internal structure or the competitive structure of their industry. This focus on how intercorporate relations limit and encourage certain types of corporate action is the basis for the bank control and hegemony theories.

Finally, class cohesion theorists assume that the ruling class is relatively homogeneous and has a common set of interests. Most of these theorists stress the common background and social interaction within the ruling class. These theorists tend to play down the different structural positions of various segments of the ruling class. In particular, critiques have charged that there are distinct differences between finance and industrial capitalists (Fitch and Oppenheimer, 1970).

Bank Control Theory

A third group of theorists argue that banks play a pivotal role in influencing the performance of corporations. A basic premise of bank control theorists is that capitalist development leads to greater centralization and concentration of production (Hilferding, [1910] 1981; Lenin, 1917). Concentration and centralization of the economy expands capital requirements, forcing corporations to increasingly rely on external sources of capital. As Shepherd (1970:93) points out, "money is more than just another input, along with labor, raw materials, and semifinished goods. Access to capital is a key source of market power, or of new entry to destroy it. Therefore, the conditions in financial markets may influence competitive possibilities throughout the economy."

Bank control theorists posit a dialectical relationship between the financial system and market economies. Increased use of capital inputs and increasing size of production units contribute to centralization in the banking system (Weeks, 1981). A centralized banking system can more easily assemble the necessary idle capital and meet the capital requirements of large producers. At the same time, banking centralization facilitates technological development and concentration of production. Hilferding ([1910] 1981:98) suggests, however, that industrial concentration is at the root of the relationship.

Surprisingly, there have been few studies of

corporate dependency on financial institutions. In one study on this issue, Lintner (1966) shows that U.S. corporations rely substantially on external sources of capital.

> This situation clearly means that nonfinancial corporations must look to financial intermediaries for the bulk of their outside, long-term debt financing. Moreover, the supply of such money for bonds and private placements is in fact dominated by a limited number of the very largest insurance companies and pension funds. Financial intermediaries have always been a more important source of outside debt capital for large nonfinancial corporations than for the smaller borrowing units, and, if anything, the dominance of a limited number of large intermediaries as a source of debt financing for the largest nonfinancial corporations, of particular concern to Berle and Means, is even greater today than in previous decades (p. 193).

Although few studies show this dependence of nonfinancial corporations on financial institutions, an abundance of data demonstrates increased indebtedness in the United States. Magdoff and Sweezy (1982) present evidence for the period from 1965 to 1985 illustrating the financial explosion in the U.S. economy. Outstanding debt across the entire economy increased by 742 percent during those years. The growth in indebtedness was somewhat uneven among sectors. For example, outstanding debt increased 586 percent by the government (including local, state, and federal governments), 697 percent by consumers, 762 percent by nonfinancial corporations, and 1920 percent by financial firms.

Bank control theorists argue that dependency of large corporations on external sources of credit places financial institutions in a powerful position (Fitch and Oppenheimer, 1970; Mintz and Schwartz, 1985). Not only does dependency on financial institutions reduce the autonomy of firms, but it also produces differential interests between the two groups. Each is concerned with maximizing profits.

Kotz (1978) points to two other forms of financial control: director interlocks and stock ownership. Director interlocks between financial and nonfinancial corporations provide a basic network for banks to coordinate the activities of firms (Levine, 1972;

Mariolis, 1978). Financial institutions are frequently
found at the center, or hub, of corporate networks,
enabling them to impose their interests on nonfinancial
corporations. The second form of control is based on
financial institutions' control of stock in nonfinancial
corporations, primarily in the form of bank trusts and
insurance pension funds. In reviewing the evidence of
bank control, Kotz concludes:

> Financial control, which was so widely recognized in
> the early part of the century, remains an important
> form of control over large nonfinancial corporations
> in the present. In the post-World War II period,
> bank trust department assets, the main basis of the
> power of financial institutions today, have been
> growing rapidly. A comparison of Berle and Means'
> results, Larner's results, and my results suggests
> that owner-control has been declining in
> importance. If both of these trends continue, and
> unless some counteracting trends develop, one would
> expect financial control to become still more
> widespread among nonfinancial corporations in the
> future (1978:118).

Stock ownership in nonfinancial corporations provides
banks and insurance companies with direct and indirect
power. Obviously, control of stock enables financial
institutions, in many cases, to influence policies and
goals of nonfinancial firms. Stock ownership provides
other forms of indirect power, such as the threat of
dumping stock (Glasberg, 1981; Glasberg and Schwartz,
1983). Financial institutions can influence the price of
stock by dumping it in the market, influencing the
likelihood for takeover. Corporate managers interested
in preventing mergers or takeovers will most likely make
decisions in the interests of the stockholders.
Kotz (1978) evaluates the evolution of financial
control over corporations through four different periods
from 1865 to the present. Banker control emerged at the
close of the Civil War because of the rapid expansion of
railroads. This expansion required the financing and
services of investment banks. Investment bankers
encouraged consolidation of the railroad systems, a
reduction in the competitive behavior among companies,
and the establishment of a monopolistic rate structure.
From 1915 to 1929, the changing structure of the
American economy produced reduced financial control in

some sectors and enhanced control in others. Financial
control was extended over large manufacturing, railroad,
and power utility corporations.

The power of financial institutions declined during
the Depression. The initial economic problems had a
particularly harsh effect on financial institutions and
the political response to the Depression weakened
financial institutions even further (Kotz, 1978:51). The
period following World War II was marked by a resurgence
of financial power. Financial institutions increased
their share of external funds supplied to nonfinancial
corporations, from about one-third in the period before
the Depression to almost two-thirds in the 1950s
(Goldsmith, 1968).

Criticism of Bank Control Theory. Major criticisms
of bank control theory have concerned the way these
theorists conceptualize corporate power (Mintz and
Schwartz, 1985). First, there are no systematic data
showing that banks frequently intervene in corporate
decision making. The evidence tends to be anecdotal and
focuses on intervention only under certain conditions.
For example, Glasberg (1985) examines the role of finance
capital during a period of corporate crisis. Presumably,
bank control is enhanced during such periods. However,
the conditions under which bank control is possible have
not been specified by researchers.

Second, there is no evidence indicating that trust
departments can actually be used to influence decision
making. Third, bank control theorists' assumption of
different interests between finance and industrial
capitalists has not been empirically tested.[4]

Bank Hegemony Theory

Several researchers (Glasberg, 1985; 1987; Green,
1986; Mintz and Schwartz, 1985) have revised bank control
theory. The revision is based largely on a synthesis of
class cohesion and bank control theories.

On the one hand, these analysts argue for the primacy
of finance capital as a unique resource monopolized
by a handful of co-acting banks and insurance
companies. This command of capital flows confers
upon the leaders of these institutions the authority
to mold the broad contours of coordinated corporate
action to their own interests. On the other hand,

bank hegemony theorists see direct control as epiphenomenal; the dominance of financial institutions is largely enacted through the mechanism that class cohesion theorists focus upon. The resulting coordination is looser and more problematic than that predicted by bank control theory, though more coherent than that predicted by class cohesion theory (Glasberg and Schwartz, 1983:318).

The key difference between the bank control theory and bank hegemony theory concerns the way in which corporate control is conceptualized. Bank control theorists focus on the variety of forms of control that enable banks to influence corporate decision making; bank hegemony theorists assume that this control is more indirect and is rarely used. Bank hegemony theorists analyze how banks define which activities and investments are considered profitable and which are risky. Financial institutions rarely exert direct influence over firms operating within these limits. This concept of "limits" not only refers to decisions, but also to nondecisions (Bachrach and Baratz, 1963).

Hegemony is used by these theorists in a different way from how is normally used in sociology. Gramsci's (1971) concept of hegemony has most often been used in an ideological sense. Sallach (1974:41) defines hegemony as the "ability to define the parameters of legitimate discussion and debate over alternative beliefs, values, and world views." Bank hegemonic theorists adopt a structural view of hegemony (Glasberg and Schwartz, 1983), focusing on how control of capital flows places constraints on corporate decision making. Under most circumstances, banks do not influence day-to-day corporate activities. Through control of capital flows, financial institutions influence decisions regarding technological development, mergers, relocation, and expansion. As Mintz and Schwartz (1985) argue,

It is our contention that structural constraint, rather than strategic intervention, is the main means by which such coordination is achieved. Though the equation of forces that produce asymmetrical interdependence may express themselves on occasion as intervention, they can also develop into hegemonic constraint that accomplishes much the same result (p. 38).

Aronson (1977) distinguishes among direct, circumventing, and indirect bank influences. According to Aronson, the influence of banks continues to grow with the maturation of the world monetary system. That influence, however, tends to be more indirect and circumventing than direct. Direct power or influence includes lobbying the legislative or the executive branch of government, rotating bank officials into government positions, and publicly calling for changes in policy. Aronson (p. 19) defines circumventing influence as involving evasion of policies and legislation in order to ensure profitability, competitive position, and planning stability for the bank and its customers. By circumventing regulations, banks force government officials to change policies and corporate actors to respond to these changes. Banks frequently exert indirect influence by altering the flow of capital in ways inconsistent with the policies of governments or international monetary agencies. Channels often used to accomplish this influence are Eurocurrency markets and actions in foreign exchange. For example, Euromarkets have been used to exert pressure on exchange rates and push governments to make monetary reform agreements. Aronson (1977) suggests that these different types of control or influence have important implications.

> Direct influence is by necessity intentional. Circumventing behavior involves the purposeful evasion of regulations but may or may not be designed to influence government policies and choices. Similarly, indirect influence may be wielded intentionally or be a side effect of banks' efforts to protect their position and profits (p. 19).

Bank hegemony theorists are seldom concerned with the intentions of bankers, but instead examine the consequences of the behavior of financial institutions for the state, corporations, and workers. Although the reasoning behind the actions of finance capitalists is important, the consequences of those actions are exceptionally important.

Bank control and bank hegemony theorists also disagree over the segmentation of interests between financial and industrial capitalists; bank control theorists contend the two have different interests and bank hegemony theorists argue their interests are essentially the same. This conceptual difference over the internal structure of the capitalist class has important implications for the conceptualization of the performance of nonfinancial firms. Bank control theorists contend that financial firms pressure nonfinancial firms to maximize short-term profits, possibly at the expense of the welfare of the nonfinancial firm. On the other hand, bank hegemony theorists argue that banks and insurance companies are concerned primarily with the long-term profits of nonfinancial firms and intervene to secure this goal in periods of crisis. According to bank hegemony theorists, finance and industrial capitalists maximize profits, but frequently disagree over whether costs and benefits should be considered in the long run or the short run.

In terms of its macroeconomic effects, bank hegemony produces a form of development whereby capital flows into the economic sectors, regions, or nations finance capitalists consider most profitable. Under most circumstances, the direction of the capital flow is not influenced directly by stockholders or bankers. Instead, finance capitalists establish a loose set of parameters that guide capital flows. As a result, some economic sectors, regions, and nations develop more rapidly than others. Bank hegemony theorists do not see development occurring through an invisible hand or by the direct control of bankers or capitalists, but through a hegemonic process that indirectly defines what is considered a good investment and which locations are considered "safe" and "reasonable." These theorists recognize, however, that financial institutions do consider social and political factors in these decisions. Thus, although financial institutions are seeking to maximize profits, they may act in ways that are narrowly defined as profit maximization.

The bank hegemony position appears to overcome many of the problems researchers encounter in examining corporate control. Dependency of nonfinancial firms on financial institutions rarely yields direct control. Analysis of corporate control requires understanding the social, political, and economic context of corporate decision making and the changing relationship between finance and industrial capital. Debates over whether banks exert direct or indirect influence have been replaced by examinations of the structural conditions that facilitate finance capitalists' influence and the relationship between finance capital and the state.

My position regarding the relationship between
finance and industrial capitalists differs somewhat from
other bank hegemony theorists. One of the major tenets
of bank hegemony theory is that finance capitalists are
concerned primarily with maximizing long-term profits.
Conflicts may develop between finance and industrial
capitalists because of the competitive pressures to
maximize short-term profits industrial capitalists face.
These theorists tend to see financial institutions as
playing a rationalizing function in advanced capitalist
societies. As financial institutions play this role,
they provide cohesion and direction for the ruling class,
which enables the ruling-class to pursue their long-term
interests.

Such a position appears to be untenable given the
rapid growth in indebtedness over the past few decades
and the lack of investment in productive facilities in
the United States. Much of the indebtedness incurred by
nonfinancial firms has not gone to improve efficiency or
productivity, but has promoted paper entrepreneurialism
and acquisitions. The recent surge in acquisitions and
take-overs would not have been possible without the
expansion of credit.

Some may interpret these changes as beneficial to the
ruling class. Such an analysis, however, ignores the
damage these structural changes have created for U.S.
corporate competitiveness in the world economy. Even the
business media have recognized the potential long-term
problems with the development of the "hollow corporation"
and the promotion of paper entrepreneurialism in the U.S.
economy. In this sense, finance capital has promoted
conditions that may undermine the long-term profitability
of the U.S. economy.

Magdoff and Sweezy (1987) recognize the active role
of the financial system in advanced capitalist societies
and link these activities to economic crises.

> What is especially striking in the present situation
> is that the more the financial system has moved away
> from its role as facilitator of the production and
> distribution of goods and services, the more it has
> taken on a life of its own, a fact that can be seen
> most vividly in the mushrooming of speculative
> activity, which is closely tied in with the debt
> explosion of the last ten years, as well as the day-
> to-day operations of financial firms (p. 20).

Therefore, I argue that finance capital does not have a rationalizing effect on capitalism, but tends to promote instability and crisis. To make this argument, I need to establish the link between the nature of corporate control and economic crises in capitalism.

Corporate Control: A Summary

Debates over ownership and control in advanced capitalist societies focus primarily on the relationship among stockholders, management, and finance capitalists. Managerial theorists contend that managers in large corporations are autonomous and tend to maximize goals other than profit. Class cohesion theorists posit that the ruling class maintains its control in large corporations by structuring management decision making. Class cohesion theorists usually take one of two positions regarding the relationship between the ruling class and financial institutions. The first position is that large corporations are not dependent on finance capital because they are able to meet their capital needs through retained earnings. There is some evidence to suggest that this situation no longer exists (Lintner, 1966). The second position is that capital is simply another resource on which firms must depend (Aldrich, 1979; Aldrich and Pfeffer, 1976). According to these theorists, resource dependency of firms does not necessarily confer providers with power in a sociological sense. The bank control and bank hegemonic theorists contend that capitalist development increases demand for capital, placing financial institutions in a pivotal position. Capital is unlike any other resource and provides financial institutions with potential influence. Bank hegemonic theorists assume that under most circumstances banks will not need to exert their influence.

My discussion of the various positions regarding ownership and control of large corporations suggests that the managerial revolution thesis has received little empirical support and is based on a rather simplistic notion of power and control (Zeitlin, 1974). The substantial disagreement between class cohesion and bank control theorists (Fitch and Oppenheimer, 1970; O'Connor, 1972; Herman, 1973) is based on methodological issues rather than substantive ones. The major disagreement concerns whether power should be conceptualized structurally, as class cohesion theorists emphasize, or instrumentally, as bank control theorists argue. In addition, bank control and class cohesion theorists tend to disagree about the class interests of finance capitalists; bank control theorists contend that finance capitalists have interests different from industrial capitalists.

Bank hegemony theorists overcome this debate by synthesizing the two positions. Bank hegemony theorists view banks and insurance companies as structuring corporate decision making through control of capital flows. The bank hegemony perspective addresses more completely than previous perspectives the methodological and empirical issues raised in the literature on corporate control. However, the perspective treats capitalist financial institutions as if they were neutral institutions. Thus far, the bank hegemony position has lacked a structural analysis of capital flows in the accumulation process. In the following section I argue that financial institutions in capitalism take on a particular form independent of those controlling the institutions.

FINANCE CAPITAL, ECONOMIC GROWTH, AND DEVELOPMENT

Although there is disagreement in the literature over the relationship between bankers and industrialists and their relative importance, there is consensus over the division in activities or functions between banks and industry. An important consequence of the development of the banking system in capitalist societies is that control over surplus value is detached from the units of production. As a result, credit becomes a commodity, albeit a somewhat different type of commodity. The commodity basis of credit exacerbates the tendency toward uneven development. In its role as an intermediary between savers and borrowers, the financial system functions as a social clearinghouse for capital, expanding and channeling capital's accumulation through its unique ability to create money capital. As the financial system collects money income, it distributes money capital to various industries, regions, and nations. Drawing on Marx's ([1894] 1981) discussion of credit, I argue that there is a tendency for the credit system to become more centralized; this centralization

has important consequences for the flow of capital. A
more centralized credit system is less likely to allocate
capital to lagging industries, regions, or nations.

Functions of Capitalist Credit Systems

De Brunhoff (1973) argues that a developed credit
system is a result of capitalist production. Although
credit existed among precapitalist societies, it takes on
a qualitatively different character within the capital
accumulation process. Credit plays an important social
function by linking production and consumption activities
and forming the basis of interaction among producers
(Brett, 1983). Among its various contributions to
accumulation, the credit system provides capitalists with
the necessary capital to invest in land- and labor-saving
technologies. The availability of credit thereby
increases profits for capitalists, which explains
industrial capitalists' willingness to share profits with
finance capitalists. The credit system also plays an
important role in the transition of societies from low
levels of economic development to advanced forms of
production (Gerschenkron, 1962).

The credit system performs two interrelated
functions in capitalist societies: (1) it serves as an
intermediary between savers and borrowers, and (2) it
becomes a mechanism for increasing the turnover rate of
capital. First, banks collect money income from all
classes and make it available as money capital. To
attract money income, banks must provide an incentive--in
most cases, the payment of interest. All capitalists
also agree to share their profit with banks because
credit becomes a critical resource in advanced
capitalism. Because of the escalating capital needs and
the adoption of land- and labor-saving technologies,
capitalists must rely increasingly on commercial banks.
Retained earnings generally do not provide a sufficient
amount of capital for large-scale production.

Workers share their income with commercial banks to
receive interest payments. Interest payments to workers
are a form of wage revenue and are considered equivalent
to variable capital (Harris, 1976). Workers also deposit
earnings in commercial banks because they depend on
credit to provide the means of reproduction, such as home
and consumer loans. By supplying consumer loans to
workers, banks fulfill an essential function for

capitalists by providing the means of reproduction that cannot be obtained through savings. Workers have become increasingly dependent on credit to obtain homes and expensive consumer goods.

As the credit system assembles and concentrates money income, it acts as a social clearinghouse by distributing the converted money capital to producers, industries, and regions (Weeks, 1981). Through the development of the credit system, the social character of capital is mediated and realized. The allocation of credit is not based solely on the risk of the potential borrower, but also on the risk of alternative investments.

The second function of a capitalist credit system is that it lets the available supply of money credit do a larger volume of work than would be possible in the absence of credit (Hilferding, [1910] 1981:89). The banking system accomplishes this feat by creating additional money capital through its ability to lend out more capital than it actually holds in deposits. Because credit permits capital to rotate more rapidly, the number of cycles through which a single sum of money capital can pass is increased. The average rate of profit decreases if capital is tied up and capitalists are unable to take advantage of more profitable investments. The extension of credit encourages the adoption of technology, the expansion of production beyond what would be possible in the absence of credit, and overspeculation.

Consequences of Credit for Development

The development of the credit system has two major effects on the accumulation process: (1) it reduces the number and length of interruptions in the circuit of capital, and (2) it contributes to the concentration of capital.[5] Marx (1981) argues that the turnover rate of capital directly influences the rate of profit; a lengthy turnover rate reduces profits because capital is tied up for long periods of time during which it could be used for more profitable purposes.

Hilferding ([1910] 1981:93) points to another advantage of using credit under unfavorable market conditions. Under those conditions, capitalists may sell below the production price without diminishing the profits of their own capital. Capitalists may retain their market share during recessions or depressions because they are not forced to make an average profit from the borrowed capital. In this instance, the return on borrowed capital does not have to be as high as capital from retained earnings.

Credit may contribute to higher industrial concentration. Banks often encourage horizontal and vertical mergers to reduce their risks. By encouraging the expansion of production through the provision of credit, banks encourage firms to take larger shares of their markets. Hilferding observes this relationship between the centralization of banks and industry:

> The development of capitalist industry produces concentration of banking, and this concentrated banking system is itself an important force in attaining the highest stage of capitalist concentration in cartels and trusts . . . For example, a number of banks have an interest in the amalgamation of steel concerns, and they work together to bring about this amalgamation even against the will of individual manufacturers ([1910] 1981:223).

Hilferding explains the rationale for this relationship between banking and industry:

> When competition in an industry is eliminated there is, first of all, an increase in the rate of profit, which plays an important role. When the elimination of competition is achieved by a merger, an undertaking is created which can count upon higher profits, and these profits can be capitalized and constitute promoter's profit. With the development of trusts this process becomes important in two respects. First, its realization constitutes a very important motive for the banks to encourage monopolization; and second, a part of the promoter's profit can be used to induce reluctant but significant producers to sell their factories, by offering a higher purchase price, thus facilitating the establishment of the cartel ([1910] 1981:223).

Finally, the provision of credit speeds up adoption of capital-intensive technologies, often leading to higher industrial concentration. The development of new technologies creates barriers to new entry because of the high cost of credit (Shepherd, 1970). Moreover, the increased cost of credit resulting from technological

development may vary for different size firms (Archer and
Faeber, 1966; Schellhardt, 1983). Hussein describes this
unique role of the credit system in the following manner:

> when finance capital is dominant the effect of the
> unevenness in the rate of profit earned by firms is
> doubly magnified: firms earning higher rates of
> profit grow faster not only because of a faster
> increase in the volume of money capital at their
> disposal but also because . . . they have easier
> access to credit compared to the firms earning lower
> rates of profit (1976:11).

The tendency for the credit system to lead to
overproduction and excessive speculation is because of
the availability of credit. At a certain level of
development, credit becomes a necessity, imposed on
producers by the competitive struggle (Weeks, 1981). If
other producers do not have equal access to sources of
credit, or must pay a higher price for the use of credit,
then a superprofit can be realized. Of course, a number
of other factors may reduce the relative importance of
access to and cost of credit, such as the ability of
producers to provide capital from retained earnings or
their ability to obtain it from the state.

Because credit contributes to increased profits, the
demand for it increases significantly with development.
Weeks (1981) argues that as a credit system develops,
exchange becomes increasingly independent of money. The
result is a pyramiding of credit with no theoretical
limit. This pyramiding establishes the basis of a crisis
where a strict separation of banks and industry exists.

The structural separation of banks and industry
typical in the U.S. economy is not maintained in all
capitalist societies; the most notable exception is
Japan. The Japanese economy is structured with banks at
the center of horizontally integrated industrial groups
(keiretsu). The banks lend money to firms in their
industrial group, and therefore, become tied to the fate
of these firms. In addition to this structural
arrangement, the bank's loans are guaranteed against
default. This intimate relationship between banks and
industry has had important consequences for the
performance of the Japanese economy. Brenner (1986)
contends that this relationship has permitted Japanese
firms to rely to a greater extent on debt than equity to
finance development than has been the case for U.S.

firms. According to Brenner (p. 22), this arrangement has placed Japanese firms at a considerable competitive advantage over U.S. firms. Japanese enterprises rely on financing to a much greater extent than U.S. firms, and they obtain these loans at two-thirds the cost of U.S. manufacturing firms (Brenner, 1986:22).

I have made two essential points in this section. First, credit plays an important role in the capital accumulation process. In its structural position as a "switching device" for capital flows, the financial system influences the rate and character of economic development. Second, in advanced capitalism, finance capital directly influences competition and profitability among firms. Because finance institutions attempt to reduce their risk and increase their profits, they will encourage increased concentration and centralization in the economy.[6] This discussion suggests that the financial system is not a passive institution that simply directs capital to the most profitable outlets. Instead, the financial system mediates the class character of capitalism and exacerbates the tendencies toward uneven development.

CORPORATE CONTROL AND UNEVEN DEVELOPMENT

In this chapter, I have integrated the literature on corporate control with the literature on the role of finance capital in producing economic growth. Most analyses of finance capital have focused exclusively on the relationship between bankers and industrial capitalists. I have argued that the bank hegemony perspective best captures the relationship between finance and industrial capital. Rather than directly controlling corporate behavior, banks define parameters on corporate activities and investments. As a result, banks influence the flow of capital between industries, regions, or nations. By defining what is considered an acceptable risk or a profitable investment, financial institutions define indirectly the course that capital takes in development.

Through its influence over capital flows, finance capital plays an important role in the accumulation process and in industrial and political change. In this sense, finance capital is an agent of social transformation, often indirectly contributing to structural changes in the economy through its form of corporate control. Through its ability to channel capital flows, financial institutions can influence social movements and political struggle. For example, increasing corporate dependency on external sources of capital enables financial institutions to influence the relationship between capital and labor.

Finally, this discussion suggests that the inherent characteristics of capitalist credit have important implications for the character of economic development. The expansion of the credit system promotes speculation and overproduction. In addition, the development of the credit system encourages centralization and concentration of the economy. Structural changes in the credit system (i.e., centralization and concentration) exacerbate the tendencies of the credit system and influence the allocation of credit in the economy. In addition, centralization and concentration of the financial system will increase the vulnerability and instability of the credit system and the rest of the economy.

This is a structural analysis of the role of finance capital in promoting uneven development. A more complete analysis of finance capital must be historical, taking into consideration the influences of class struggle and the state on capital flows. Prior to this historical analysis, I examine the structural relationship of the state to finance capital.

NOTES

1. There is considerable debate concerning whether these theorists, particularly Hilferding, saw finance capital as a final stage of capitalism (see Sweezy [1942] for a discussion of this issue).

2. Marxists differ with respect to their conceptualization of the interrelationship between finance and industrial capitalists. Lenin (1917), for example, saw the two groups as merging under the period of finance capital. Hilferding ([1910] 1981), on the other hand, argued that finance capitalists were separate from industrial capitalists, although financial institutions frequently own stock in nonfinancial corporations.

3. Class cohesion theorists tend to take one of two positions regarding the nature of corporate power. Some

see class cohesion as an empirical process, where the ruling class directly structures decisions. Other theorists see corporate control as an outcome or a structure, or both. Most of the discussion of class cohesion position will refer to the first interpretation. The second interpretation comes much closer to the bank hegemony position discussed later in the chapter.

4. There has been considerable debate in the literature over this matter. See the debate in <u>Socialist Revolution</u> (Fitch and Oppenheimer, 1970; O'Connor, 1972) for an excellent review of the issues.

5. It is difficult to separate the effects of banks and the structural logic of capital accumulation on the tendency for concentration and centralization in capitalist economies. The two factors may be highly interrelated as the expansion of banking capital facilitates greater concentration and centralization of the economy.

6. Large banks and more centralized credit systems will consider more carefully the risk and costs of loaning to smaller firms also. Much of the increased cost of loaning to smaller firms is associated with the transaction costs of loans.

3

Capital Flows and the Capitalist State

In this chapter I focus on the relationship between finance capital and the state--on both how the state directly and indirectly influences capital flows and how finance capital provides constraints for state action. Recent analyses of the capitalist state suggest that the state's control over capital flows has become increasingly important in its effort to promote accumulation and to improve efficiency and productivity. The structure of financial markets, however, limits the state's ability to control capital flows. The highly specialized nature of financial markets, the large number of financial institutions, and the division between finance and commerce make it difficult for the state to use capital markets to direct industrial change. Deregulation of financial institutions will promote a more centralized credit system and enhances the state's ability to negotiate with finance capital over the direction and magnitude of capital flows. I examine the political and economic forces that contributed to financial deregulation and the consequences not only for state industrial policy, but also for the structure of the credit system. Although deregulation provides a more centralized credit system through which the state can direct technological and industrial change, it also increases the volatility of local capital markets and restricts the capacity of the state to implement industrial policies producing further economic growth. Thus, financial deregulation will contribute to structural problems in the economy.

THE CAPITALIST STATE

The state has been the topic of much recent debate among social scientists. There appears to be a growing consensus among neo-Marxists and neo-Weberians that pluralist accounts of state policy fail to consider the structure of power in the state and society. Neo-Marxists and neo-Weberians differ, however, on the extent to which they believe the state is autonomous of society.[1] Neo-Marxists argue that the state is shaped by the class structure of society and that it functions to reproduce class relations in capitalist society. Skocpol (1985) identifies three broad approaches in this literature: instrumentalism, political functionalism, and the class-struggle position.

Instrumentalists contend that the ruling class directly influences the state apparatus. State policies reflect the economic interests of the ruling class, as a result of either direct representation in the state apparatus or the special interest process (Domhoff, 1983). Domhoff's work is an exemplar of the instrumentalist position. Domhoff argues that the ruling class is a demarcated social class having power over the state apparatus and the underlying population. The power elite is the operating arm of the ruling class and is actively involved in controlling major social and economic institutions and dominating governmental processes. Domhoff demonstrates that an upper class remains dominant in the U.S.; there is enough unity among members of the class and it is a governing class.

Political functionalists (also called structuralists) assert that the capitalist state must secure the conditions for capital accumulation (Poulantzas, 1974). The state is conceptualized as "relatively autonomous," yet it operates in a manner that guarantees a good business climate. Dependence of the state on corporate profits and capital markets for revenue provides an incentive for state managers to promote conditions for accumulation. For Poulantzas, the state does not directly represent the dominant classes' economic interests, but is the center for political power and is an organizing agent of political struggle. In this sense, the state functions to organize the dominant classes and splinters the dominated classes.

Carnoy (1984) argues that the instrumentalist-structuralist debate centers primarily on methods and epistemology rather than substance. Instrumentalists

focus on the ruling class's influence on the state;
structuralists examine the constraints on state policy.
This debate has been eclipsed by a more historically
informed position, the class-struggle position, that
assumes that the state may operate in an instrumentalist
manner some times, and in a structural fashion at other
times. I adopt the class-struggle position in this
chapter and demonstrate how state policy, capital flows,
and class-struggle.

Class-struggle theorists consider the state a
mediator of class conflict and give the state much more
autonomy. They believe it is possible to have a social
policy that benefits dominated classes and protects the
long-run interests of the capitalist class. Thus, state
policy is a part of the economic and political struggles
in society. This position differs from the pluralist
theories because it recognizes differential power of
groups in society and the limitations of state policy.
In addition, the class-struggle position assumes that
state policy must be understood historically.

Although debate continues on this matter, the class-
struggle position appears to be most consistent with the
principles of historical materialism and resists the
development of a generalized theory of the state. Class-
struggle theories avoid the subjectivistic tendencies of
the instrumentalist theories of the state and the
inverted functionalism of the structuralist-functionalist
position (Block, 1977). In the following, I use
O'Connor's (1973) work as an exemplar of the class-
struggle position to examine the role of credit in state
policy. This topic has been ignored in much of the
literature on the relationship between the state and the
economy.

Functions of the Capitalist State

O'Connor (1973) argues that the capitalist state
performs two basic functions: accumulation and
legitimation. Corresponding to these functions is the
twofold character of state expenditures as social-capital
and social-expenditures. Social-capital expenditures are
indirectly profitable and provide the conditions for
private accumulation. The state takes on these
expenditures because they are too costly for individual
capitalists. Two different forms of social capital are
social-investment and social-consumption expenditures.

Social-investment expenditures increase the productivity of labor power. Examples of social investments are roads, public-financed industrial development parks, and public education. Social-consumption expenditures reduce the reproduction costs of labor. An example of a social-consumption expenditure is a social-insurance program, such as Medicare or Medicaid. State expenditures fulfilling the second function, legitimation, are referred to as social expenditures. These expenditures are not directly productive, but are intended to maintain social harmony. Many analysts consider the poverty programs of the 1960s an example of a social expenditure designed to reduce urban social unrest (Piven and Cloward, 1971).

Public credit, in most cases, can be considered an example of a social-capital expenditure, as either a social-investment or a social-consumption expenditure.[2] Workers must have access to credit to purchase homes and other consumer products that cannot be purchased from retained earnings (savings). Although large corporations are now providing home loans for some employees or are purchasing employees' homes when they are transferred, credit for home and consumer goods has historically come from commercial banks (Harris, 1976). In general, workers must qualify for government loans on the basis of their low incomes or some other specific need. During a crisis, the state may take a more active role in providing credit. In doing so, the state is reducing the costs of reproduction for capital (social-consumption expenditure). The state has been indirectly subsidizing housing costs for all homeowners through the income tax deduction on home loans. Thus, revenue lost because of these deductions is another form of social-consumption expenditure.

Credit the state provides to capitalists is also a social-investment expenditure. By providing capitalists with access to credit, usually at a lower cost than is available from private lenders, the state enlarges the scope of production. The provision of credit encourages capitalists to increase the productivity of labor power. For example, Barry (1981) suggests the increased availability and low cost of farm credit led to increased land prices and rapid consolidation of farms during the 1970s. Farm operators were forced to expand the size of their production unit to use efficiently the new technologies they obtained with borrowed capital. The provision of credit by the state also contributes to the

profits of monopoly capital by increasing consumption.
In other words, by providing consumers with credit, the
financial system is artificially creating demand for
consumer goods.

As I have suggested, O'Connor's (1973) argument does
not rest entirely on the economic functions of the state.
State managers undertake social expenses to reduce social
unrest and legitimate the state's economic role. State-
subsidized credit is also a response to the social unrest
and disruption of normal living patterns created by
structural problems inherent in capitalist economies.
Mooney (1986), for example, argues that the state
promoted access to agricultural credit after the Great
Depression in response to tenancy problems in the South.
Increases in the number of tenants in the 1930s led to
the rise of the Southern Tenant Farmer's Union and
ultimately to a set of New Deal farm policies easing
access to credit and encouraging land ownership (Grubbs,
1971). Increased access to credit enabled tenants to
purchase land, but contributed to some of the structural
problems in the farm economy today (see Chapter 4).
Many of the public sources of credit were created in
response to the Great Depression. Primarily intended to
eliminate barriers to the efficient flow of credit within
the commercial-credit system, these public sources of
credit were established to ensure that important social
priorities, such as private land ownership and retention,
were being met. These public sources of credit embodied
the state's contradictory functions as they were designed
to help chronically poor families and to improve market
conditions. Thus, it is often difficult to pigeonhole
many state expenditures because they contribute to
accumulation and legitimation.

This discussion suggests that these functions of the
capitalist state are often contradictory (O'Connor,
1973). As the state plays its economic role of promoting
capital accumulation it creates additional social
problems: stress on local and regional economies,
imbalances between industries and sectors, and unequal
distribution of wealth and income. These problems
require the state to expand even further through the
growth of social-capital expenses. In response to social
problems, the state often directly provides credit,
guarantees private loans, or regulates financial
institutions. This expansion of the state eventually
becomes a drag on capital accumulation because additional
revenues are required to take on new activities. These

growing contradictory demands increase social capital
expenditures and social expenditures, ultimately creating
a fiscal crisis for the state. Without dramatic
increases in growth, the state is required to cut back on
some of its expenditures. Piven and Cloward (1971)
suggest, however, that many of the state's activities
become institutionalized and regarded as essential
services of the state. As a result, the state has a
difficult time reducing expenditures in these areas. An
excellent example of this phenomenon is the Reagan
administration's attempt to reduce expenditures for
social security. The administration soon discovered that
these expenditures were considered rights that would have
severe political consequences if removed.

In this section I have outlined the various Marxist
positions regarding the relationship between the state
and society. The class-struggle position overcomes many
of the conceptual weaknesses of the political
functionalist and instrumentalist positions. State
control over capital flows is critical to the
accumulation and legitimation functions of the state.
The state's ability to influence capital flows is,
however, problematical. In the following section, I
examine the relationship between the state and the
financial system. This relationship will define the
ability of the state to direct economic markets and
industrial change.

FINANCIAL SYSTEMS, THE STATE, AND MARKETS

Most researchers examining the role of the state in
providing the conditions for accumulation have assumed
that this intervention is even and unproblematic. The
state is seen as rationalizing market economies and
providing a mechanism for introducing long-run interests
into the market. The state's ability to intervene in
market economies, however, depends on a number of
historical and institutional factors such as
administrative structure of the state, industrial
structure, and prevailing political coalitions. The
financial system is also a key institutional factor
mediating the relationship between the state and markets.
Although all of these factors interact to influence the
state's intervention into markets, I focus primarily on
how financial systems interact with state structure to
produce certain outcomes. I argue that financial systems

facilitate and constrain the state's economic policy.

Zysman (1983) outlines three types of financial systems; each has different consequences for the relationships between the financial system, the state, and markets. The three systems differ with respect to the competitive structure of capital markets and the ability of the state to direct capital flows. The three systems are (1) one based on capital markets, (2) a credit-based system with market interrelations dominated by state-administered prices, and (3) a credit-based system in which a limited number of financial institutions dominate.

Under the first system, banks, firms, and governments are in distinct spheres (p. 70). Capital markets are relatively competitive, with a large number of specialized financial institutions. A highly specialized market is evidenced by a variety of capital sources other than commercial banks. Specialization among financial institutions prevents any segment of finance capital from becoming dominant and developing a unified stance toward industrial capital; financial institutions are limited in their ability to influence nonfinancial firms directly. This structure, however, does not preclude financial institutions from indirectly influencing corporate decision-making. The state under this system is unable to direct the allocation of credit to different economic sectors. Zysman argues that Britain and the United States exemplify this model. Although the U.S. has had extremely specialized financial markets and a large number of financial institutions, this structure is rapidly changing in the period of financial deregulation.

The second model is based on state-administered prices. Nonfinancial firms do not have as many choices within capital markets, so they must turn to commercial banks. Finance capital is relatively unified under this model. The state directly facilitates money creation and administers prices for credit. One consequence of this system is that finance capital becomes a direct link between the state and markets. Control over capital flows is an important instrument that the state can use to promote industrial change.

It appears that government's role is to compensate for weaknesses in an existing private financial system. Historically, the state intervenes to accomplish particular purposes and the resulting financial structure institutionalizes its

discretionary influence in the financial market. The
political implication is that the state's
entanglement with industry becomes part and parcel of
the financial system. The borderline between public
and private blurs, not simply because of political
arrangements, but because of the very structure of
the financial markets (Zysman, 1983:72).

The French and Italian systems closely resemble this
model.
    The third model is also credit based, with a few
financial institutions dominating the system. Prices are
not determined by administrative action, as in the second
model, but by concentrated financial power. The state
has few, if any, mechanisms with which it can effectively
influence capital flows or the price of credit.
Financial institutions influence corporations through
their market power. The state is unable to guide the
allocation of credit directly, but banks may serve as
policy allies for the state (Zysman, 1983:72). Zysman
suggests that the German system is the best example of
this third model.
    Zysman's typology allows us to examine the variety of
structural constraints the state faces as it attempts to
influence the flow of capital and how finance capital
places constraints on industrial policy. In a system
based on capital markets, the state conflicts with
financial institutions and nonfinancial firms as it
attempts to intervene in the market and promote
industrial change. The capital market system does not
permit the state to make market changes in response to
social needs. As Zysman suggests, a capital market-based
system isolates finance, industry, and the state, and
makes it difficult, if not impossible, for the state to
promote industrial change.

> In a system characterized by financial allocation
> according to market-established prices, an elaborated
> capital market, and limited industrial dependence on
> long-term debts, the state will encounter financial
> institutions as rivals defending the existing
> organization of the financial system and will
> confront financial markets as barriers to state
> influence in industry. The struggle to establish
> interventionist instruments or state-led industrial
> promotion can easily degenerate into a conflict over
> the sanctity of markets (p. 81).

In a credit-based system with state-administered prices, the state is aided by finance capital in its effort to gain support for state-led industrial promotion (Zysman, 1983:80). Under this system, the state can most easily direct capital flows and investment in industry, regions, and so on. Under the third model, a credit-based system with a limited number of financial institutions dominating the market, the state may be able to negotiate with financial institutions to regulate economic activity.

From this discussion we can see that the institutional structure of finance capital in the United States presents obstacles for state intervention in the economy. The large number of banks and the variety of financial institutions limit the state's ability to direct investment and corporate behavior. Economic problems in the United States in the 1970s initiated a change in the relationship between financial institutions and the state. This relationship between finance capital and the state is currently being restructured through the deregulation of the banking system. This change reflects a shift from Zysman's first model to the third. The result will be a more centralized financial system, but one that does not enable the state to direct industrial change to any greater extent. Instead, these changes will enlarge the power of finance capital. In the following section, I examine how banking deregulation is influencing financial markets and the state's capacity for economic intervention.

DEREGULATION, ORGANIZATIONAL STRUCTURE, AND CAPITAL MARKETS

During the Depression, major reforms were enacted to limit commercial banks' sphere of influence and control.[3] At the time, the public perceived the banks to be the major contributors to the Depression (Burns, 1974). These banking regulations established the scope of permissible activities, cost of services, and geographical limitations to expansion. One of the most important pieces of legislation was the Glass-Steagall Act of 1933, which forced commercial banks out of the investment-banking business. This act effectively created a division between commerce and finance in this country.

Owens (1986) indicates several rationales for the state to regulate the financial system: regulation (1) expands the financial power of government, which generates taxation revenues; (2) reduces externalities that influence control of the macro economy, (3) ensures financial solvency, (4) maximizes competition and prevents concentration and centralization of financial and political power, (5) protects the small depositors, and (6) provides a means of allocating credit to meet certain social goals.

The Reagan Administration's attack on New Deal programs has been widespread, affecting several industries, such as transportation, communication, and agriculture.[4] At the heart of this attack have been regulations surrounding the banking industry. Recent changes in banking regulations are restructuring financial markets. These changes will have important consequences for the cost of and access to credit. Deregulation will most likely exacerbate the trends toward concentration and centralization in the economy and integrate more tightly the banking sector into national and international markets.

Several factors contributed to banking deregulation in the 1980s. High interest rates and the development of alternative investments for savings (e.g., money-market funds and certificates of deposit) put pressure on commercial banks in the late 1970s. Regulation Q placed a ceiling on the interest rates commercial banks could pay on deposits. As a result, capital flowed out of commercial banks and thrifts into alternative investments paying a higher interest rate on deposits. Money market accounts increased in popularity in the late 1970s because they offered higher interest rates than standard checking accounts. These restrictions forced many banks to shift their capital overseas.

These problems were compounded by the growth of nondepository financial institutions (Fraser and Kolari, 1985). Financial markets were invaded in the late 1970s by nonfinancial institutions, such as Sears and Merrill Lynch, offering products and services traditionally provided by financial institutions. Nonfinancial institutions had an important advantage because they were immune from most of the regulations that applied to banks and thrifts. Commercial banks were at a competitive disadvantage with these nonfinancial institutions and called for a level playing field. Financial institutions asked federal regulators to permit them to become more involved in activities not directly related to finance. A series of editorials in the Wall Street Journal in February of 1982 argued that deregulation was necessary for finance institutions to be in a position to compete against the unregulated nonbank institutions. "Free market" economists added fuel to the fire by providing additional theoretical justification for banking deregulation.

The major obstacle for financial institutions to expand their activities into these new areas was the Bank Holding Company Act of 1970, which established a "laundry list" of permissable activities. To be added to the laundry list, an activity must be closely related to banking and produce public benefits, such as greater convenience, competition, or efficiency. These benefits were expected to outweigh any possible costs, such as undue concentration of resources or unfair competition. This criterion has been applied rather loosely to applications; many activities that are not closely related to banking have been included in recent years.

Deregulation was also a response to the economic crisis in the thrift industry; regulatory changes were seen as necessary to save the industry. Regulators began allowing out-of-state commercial banks to acquire troubled savings and loans, thereby circumventing the geographic limitations.

Technological advancements in the banking industry created problems for regulators. In particular, the Automated Teller Machine (ATM) was a de facto form of branch banking. Banking networks permit users to withdraw and deposit cash almost anywhere in the country. Therefore, this technological development pushed regulators to define more carefully a "bank" and the limits of new forms of banking.

These developments led Congress to pass two laws responsible for most of the regulatory changes in the banking industry: the Depository Institutions Deregulation and Monetary Control Act of 1980 and the Garn-St. Germain Depository Institution Act of 1982. These acts focused on three basic issues. First, this legislation influenced the cost of credit and financial services. By removing the ceiling on interest rates paid to depositors, deregulation increased the interest rate charged to borrowers and the cost of providing services. Second, regulatory changes increased significantly the variety of services and activities in which financial institutions could become involved. For example, in 1982 banks and thrifts were allowed to introduce money-market deposit accounts. It is still questionable whether banks will be able to sell mutual funds and insurance in the future. Finally, deregulation has influenced the geographic limits on banking activities. In certain cases, banks have been allowed to acquire troubled banks across state lines. Regional banking systems have also been declared legal by the Supreme Court. In these arrangements, banks in one state are permitted to acquire banks in another state if the reverse is permitted. Many states have already adopted interstate banking laws.

Costs of Credit and Services

Commercial bankers argue that deregulation will make U.S. banks more competitive in a market that is increasingly influenced by Japanese and European financial institutions. As one might expect, the strongest advocates of deregulation have been the large banks. Large banks have argued that pricing restrictions and curbs on the services that banks can provide have reduced the profitability of the commercial banking industry. Critics, such as the Independent Bankers Association, argue that banking restrictions should be maintained because of the unique role commercial banks play in capitalist societies (the creation of money and credit). One of the most adamant critics of deregulation has been Henry Kaufman, an influential economist from Saloman Brothers, who argues that if we accept the idea that competition in banking should be encouraged, then we must also accept the idea that some banks will fail in the process (Judis, 1984).

Although there is little empirical evidence to evaluate the consequences of banking deregulation, we can anticipate certain outcomes. Lifting the interest rate ceiling on deposits will have several important consequences. First, deregulation provides banks with an incentive to make riskier loans, such as the oil and real estate loans made in the 1980s, to compensate for the increased cost of funds (New York Times, 1986b). The increased risk orientation of commercial banks contributes to the rapid increase in the number of banks that have failed or required financial assistance by the Federal Deposit Insurance Corporation (the largest number since the Depression). Kotz (1985) suggests that deregulation has produced a no lose situation for large banks because if they have good luck, they make high profits and if they don't, they will be bailed out by the government.

> Deregulation promotes bank failure because the deregulated environment is more competitive, and competition produces both winners and losers. One might think that once the weaker banks had folded, the system would then stabilize. But there is a deeper reason for instability. Deregulation goads banks to adopt a more aggressive profit orientation. This makes it harder to pass up the high profits promised by riskier loans and investments. But lately more and more are not repaid--the loan loss rate at the 25 largest banks tripled from 1981 to 1985. Normally the fear of losses would temper the appeal of risky investments, but federal regulatory authorities have made it clear that they will insulate depositors and even stockholders from the full costs of failure (p. 11).

This increased risk orientation of commercial banks has three important implications for the provision of credit. The increased number of risky loans made in the recent past may force banks to continue loaning to these borrowers to insure that they will not default on their loans. For example, large commercial banks in the United States have invested so much in the Third World that they cannot afford to allow these countries to default on their loans. Fewer funds may be available for other purposes and the cost of credit may be driven up for other borrowers. Another possible consequence is that regulators may force banks to be extremely cautious in the rest of their loan portfolio. This would also restrict access and increase the cost of credit to small businesses and minorities. In other words, the increased risk orientation of commercial banks will not lead to greater access to credit for risky borrowers per se, but to risky loans that are extremely profitable. Deregulation will force bankers to consider more closely the transaction costs involved in a loan, rather than its overall risk. Because of the economic problems of Third World countries, it has become increasingly difficult for them to repay their loans. One response has been for the World Bank to make an additional loans to these countries

to increase agricultural production as a means of
repaying creditors (New York Times, 1986a). Such a
strategy, however, would increase surpluses on the world
market and depress prices for American farmers.

A second consequence of lifting the interest rate
ceiling on deposits is that credit markets are now more
closely tied to national and international markets, which
has increased the volatility of rates (Hughes et al.,
1986). Increased volatility of rates should make access
to credit for small borrowers and minorities more
problematic in the future. Hughes et al. (1986) suggest
that many banks have responded to deregulation by simply
passing the higher costs on to borrowers.

Finally, deregulation is contributing to the
financial stress of small, particularly rural, banks.
Although many of the difficulties in these banks are
related to the problematic loans in agriculture, energy,
oil, and the Third World, small banks in rural areas have
also experienced stress related to increased
concentration in the industry. This stress is
contributing to an increased number of mergers, possibly
leading to a capital drain in rural areas in the future.

Geographic Limitations

A second focus of deregulation is geographical
restrictions on commercial banks. As I mentioned
earlier, among the factors leading to fewer geographical
restrictions were the emergence of "nonbank" banks and
new methods of electronic funds transfer that were not
being regulated. In addition, there was a rapid
expansion of multibank holding companies and mergers.
Hughes et al. (1986) estimate that by 1990 there will be
one-third fewer banks than there were in 1986. A key
determinant of the rate at which banks will merge is how
quickly states will adopt interstate banking laws. By
the end of 1986, 35 states had enacted legislation
providing for regional or national interstate banking.
Almost all of this expansion has occurred over the past
four years. Only a few states have nationwide banking
provisions. Alaska, Arizona, and Maine have legislation
permitting interstate banking from any state without
reciprocity requirements. Several other states have
similar legislation on the condition that they have
reciprocity privileges. Regional reciprocal laws--which
restrict access to banks from specific states--have been

developed in the Southeast, Mid-Atlantic, and Midwest states.

The increased number of mergers will likely shift control of loan decisions away from local communities. This shift in control should have important implications for the loan policies and practices of commercial banks. After acquisition, banks typically standardize and formalize many of the bank's practices by instituting maximum loan limits for loan offers and written lending policies and by appointing representatives on the bank's committees to review credit requests. Green (1984; 1986) demonstrates that when loan decisions are made outside the local community, the tendency is for loan officers to use rational-technical criteria, because there is no longer a means of evaluating the character or trustworthiness of potential borrowers. The loan evaluation process can only consider objective factors, such as the amount of collateral and cash-flow statements. Finally, as banking systems increase in size they can more objectively evaluate transaction costs and may reduce the number of less profitable loans.

New Services

The third prong of banking deregulation is the provision of services by financial institutions. Historically, there has been a clear-cut distinction between banking and commerce in the United States. This sacred boundary has been maintained because of the abuses that could arise if banks were involved in activities placing them in a conflict of interest.

Deregulation of services and activities of financial institutions may change the traditional emphasis in commercial banks on the provision of loans, particularly certain types of loans. If these new services and activities compete (in terms of profits) with loans, banks may choose to reduce the amount of capital available for loans and increase the amount available for more profitable activities and services. This shift within financial institutions would reduce access to and increase the cost of credit to borrowers, with a disproportionate impact on those industries that are considered risky.

The risky nature of many activities in which banks become involved may threaten bank profitability (Business Week, 1986b). The Federal Reserve has expressed concern

over new financial instruments, such as currency swaps,
interest-rate swaps, and certain letters of credit. The
major concern over these activities is that they are all
"off balance sheet," which means that the risks are not
evident from the bank's financial statement.

CAPITAL FLOWS AND THE STATE

New Deal banking regulations placed constraints on
pricing practices, nonbanking activities, and location of
commercial banks. These regulations became increasingly
problematic in the 1970s as domestic loans declined in
profitability and many nonfinancial corporations entered
into banking activities. To circumvent banking
regulations, money-center banks moved much of their
lending activity to overseas branches and sought to find
ways of entering into nonbank activities. The threat of
capital flight and the demand from commercial banks to
create a level playing field in financial markets led
Congress to deregulate the finance industry.[5]
As I mentioned above, one likely consequence of
banking deregulation is a more centralized banking
industry. The U.S. commercial banking industry is
somewhat of an anomaly. Most developed countries (e.g.,
Canada, Great Britain, and Switzerland) have very few
banks; four or fewer banks control more than half of the
deposits in these countries. There are about 14 thousand
banks in the United States. In 1976, 41 commercial banks
controlled 42 percent of the deposits in the United
States, compared to 28 percent in 1960 (Noyelle and
Stanback, 1984). Although the United States has a large
number of banks, a relatively small number of money-
center banks control the majority of deposits in the
country. The number of mergers and acquisitions among
banking, finance, and insurance firms has increased
dramatically over the past decade. From 1978 to 1984,
mergers and acquisitions in these industries increased
from 253 to 2,533 (Kaufman and Kormendi, 1986:160). The
value of these transactions increased from $4.1 billion
to $122.2 billion during the same time period. The
percentage of commercial bank deposits accounted for by
the largest 100 banks increased from 33.7 percent in 1925
to 51.4 percent in 1978 (Kaufman and Kormendi, 1986:166).
One recurring issue regarding the structure of the
banking industry has been lack of integration in the
system. The Federal Reserve System was intended to

provide greater integration within the monetary system by expanding or contracting credit to bring supply in line with demand. Many independent banks did not join the Federal Reserve System (and many still do not belong today). Even when small, independent banks do belong to the system, monetary controls have much less effect on their loan policies and practices than they have on large banks.

> In a nation with a large number of small banking units, many of which are not motivated by profit considerations, or which hesitate to change policies for reasons of inertia, the impact of credit control is blunted to a degree (Nadler, 1968:72).

Lamb (1962) argues that the bank holding company form of organization provided some of the benefits of a more integrated system.

> Certainly the concentration of bank management in fewer hands would smooth the process of monetary management. In group banking the aspect of unified corporate control, through common or voting stock ownership, links banks together in a manner that may permit a greater responsiveness to monetary decisions. To assert that this goal is accomplished unfailingly through bank holding company operations would disregard the absence of substantive empirical evidence. On the other hand, it is logical to maintain that the group form of banking organization does add to the effectiveness of monetary policy, if it is the desire of the concentrated bank management to do so (p. 168).

Much centralization in the banking system has resulted from the bank holding company movement. The first bank holding company was the Adam Hannah Company of Minnesota, incorporated in 1900. Several factors contributed to the bank holding company movement. There were obviously some economies of scale in this form of organization (Piper, 1971). In addition, the multibank holding company form of organization has been a preferred form of geographic expansion because of the restrictive branch banking laws. The bank holding company became a popular form of financial organization in the 1960s and early 1970s. In 1965, there were only 53 multibank holding companies (MBHCs) in the United States. These

banks controlled about 8 percent of the commercial bank
deposits in the country. By 1980, MBHCs controlled more
than 35 percent of the deposits (Watkins and West, 1982).

The 1956 Bank Holding Company Act was the first law
to effectively control the expansion of bank holding
companies (BHCs). Among its many provisions the 1956 Act
defined a BHC, required BHCs to seek approval from the
Board of Governors of the Federal Reserve System prior to
acquiring any voting shares of banks, limited acquisition
of stock in banks to those banks which were in the same
state as the central office of the BHC, and made it
unlawful for a BHC to acquire voting shares of a
nonbanking company.

The 1956 Act restricted multibank holding companies
from expanding into certain areas, but it did not legally
restrict one-bank holding companies. This loophole
opened the floodgate for a proliferation of one-bank
holding companies in the 1960s. In addition, the 1956
Act did not establish a clear set of guidelines to
evaluate applications for acquisition or merger. The Act
was operationalized in a relatively liberal manner and
the vast majority of the applications were accepted.

In an attempt to remedy these problems, Congress
amended the Bank Holding Act in 1966. One goal of the
Amendment was to clarify the relative importance of the
established criteria used for reviewing applications for
mergers. Two major loopholes remained--both bank chains
and one-bank holding companies were still exempt from
regulation. The 1966 Amendment increased some
restrictions on multibank holding companies, but
encouraged the growth of one-bank holding companies.
Some have termed the 1966 Amendment as the beginning of
the "one-bank holding company gold rush."

By 1970, one-bank holding companies were involved in
more than 100 widely diversified activities from mining,
manufacturing, agriculture, transportation to wholesale
and retail trade. Small business people who were likely
to be hurt by the expansion of one-bank holding
companies, the press, and liberal politicians called for
legislation to shore up the "loopholes."

Wright Patman, Chairman of the House Banking, Finance
and Urban Affairs Committee, led the fight to maintain
the traditional boundaries between banking and commerce.
Patman proposed a "laundry list" of permissable
activities restricting all BHCs to activities closely
related to banking. Patman introduced his highly
restrictive proposal for amending the regulations in

1969. The Nixon administration produced a bill which was significantly weaker than Patman's bill. The result of a House-Senate Conference Committee was a compromise that established a laundry list, but did not restrict BHC's nonbanking business to financial activities.

The 1970 Amendment effectively eliminated the loophole for one-bank holding companies and encouraged banks to expand through the formation of multibank holding companies. The result has been a growing concentration and centralization of capital markets over the past 25 years.

Centralization and Concentration of Markets

It is important to make the distinction between concentration and centralization at national versus local levels. The data suggest that bank deposits are becoming increasingly concentrated in national capital markets, as large money-center banks extend themselves into new markets. Kaufman and Kormendi (1986) present evidence indicating that concentration ratios for commercial banks in SMSAs and counties have generally decreased over the past 15 years. In their analysis of changes in concentration ratios of SMSAs and counties, they distinguish between expansion and nonexpansion states. Surprisingly, concentration ratios declined the most in nonexpansion states from 1966 to 1976.

This analysis suggests that national capital markets are becoming more concentrated while local capital markets are becoming less concentrated. How does one explain these different trends? One reason for this is that as money-center banks and regional banks expand, they are increasing competition in local markets. Competition on the local level, however, may only be temporary. This is a concern for all of the industries currently being deregulated. The effect of this expansion depends on how it occurs, through acquisition of existing banks or de novo. Federal regulators have preferred the latter type of expansion because it generally increases competition in the local market. At the same time, this expansion increases concentration in national capital markets. Acquisition of existing banks would tend to increase market concentration in both local and national markets.

The differing trends in concentration and centralization of capital markets may also signal the

growth of a dualistic structure within the banking
industry, with a small number of very large money-center
banks and a large number of local banks. Each segment of
the industry may play different functions, have different
customers, and compete across sectors on a very limited
basis. Under such a system, large banks would meet the
capital needs of large businesses and smaller banks would
do the same for small, local businesses. In my own
research, I have found that large multibank holding
companies are typically not interested in acquiring the
banks in the smallest towns (Green, 1985). In most
cases, they prefer to acquire banks that are near urban
centers and are immune to some of the cyclical trends
affecting the agricultural economy in rural areas.
Therefore, we should not extend the large number of
mergers to influence directly banks in the smallest
towns. In the long run, deregulation should have
devastating consequences for these banks.

Although this dualistic structure has grown over the
past few decades, deregulation is undermining the
segmentation of capital markets by linking local capital
markets to national and international capital markets
more closely. In addition, technological changes and
deregulation of financial institutions are eliminating
much of the specialization in the financial industry. A
reduction in the degree of specialization in financial
markets should drive up prices for services because there
will be less competition among various sectors of the
financial industry.

SUMMARY

In this chapter I have moved from the theoretical
discussion of finance capital in the previous chapter to
a more concrete analysis of financial markets. The major
thesis in this chapter is that the structure and
character of financial markets influences the capacity of
the capitalist state to intervene into the economy. As I
discussed in the previous chapter, financial markets are
in pivotal locations for directing industrial change in
market economies. Therefore, states that are unable to
direct financial institutions will have less capacity to
solve problems in capitalist economies.

The rise of transnational capital exacerbates the
contradictory character of capitalist credit. Increased
mobility of capital encourages overspeculation and makes

it more difficult for the state to regulate the activities of financial institutions. The shift in capital flows pressures the state to respond to the contradiction by favoring finance capital (Glasberg, 1986). As a result, the state must also respond to class conflict in a different manner.

Support for a more centralized and concentrated banking system was expressed recently by officials in the Treasury Department. Treasury officials favor the creation of "superbanks," conglomerates that would consist of large commercial banks and industrial companies (New York Times, 1987d). Treasury officials believe that superbanks would be more competitive with the large European and Japanese banks. The development of superbanks would have important consequences for the structure and performance of not only financial markets, but throughout the economy.

I began this chapter by outlining Zysman's typology of institutional arrangements between financial systems, the state, and markets. This typology suggests that the institutional arrangements in the United States constrain the state's ability to direct economic development. However, the state can restructure financial markets to facilitate their goals. Contrary to the Reagan administration's rhetoric, banking deregulation will produce less competition in the economy. By encouraging increased centralization in financial systems, the state undermines its own ability to effectively direct capital flows in the long-run.

NOTES

1.   Neo-Weberians argue that the state is much more autonomous than neo-Marxists are willing to admit. They adopt a state-centered approach, which focuses on the political activities of the state rather than its economic function. State-centered approaches often examine the institutional structure of the state and the role of political parties in the policy formulation process (Skocpol, 1985). These theorists tend to also reject previous attempts to develop a unitary theory of the state. Such an approach appears to be consistent with recent interpretations of Weber's emphasis on historical analyses.

2.   Consumer loans may put a drag on capital investment because they reduce the amount of available funds for business loans.

3.   Among the most important banking laws are: Federal Reserve Act of 1913, McFadden Act of 1927, Glass-Steagall Act of 1933, Banking Act of 1935; Federal Deposit Insurance Act of 1935, Bank Holding Company Act of 1956, and Regulation Q.

4.   Deregulation actually began during the last years of the Carter Administration and was implemented by the Reagan Treasury and the Senate Banking Committee. The Senate Committee passed legislation in 1980 and 1982, which restructured banking regulations.   It should be pointed out that banking deregulation was accelerated by the Reagan Treasury's liberal interpretation of the Glass-Steagall Act.

5.   Deregulation has apparently slowed the shift of capital overseas somewhat, but not entirely.   Saulsbury (1986:7) reports that U.S. banking assets overseas total $458 billion, a tenfold increase since 1970.   He indicates, "expansion abroad continues, and at a faster rate than is suggested by the available data" (p. 7).

4

The Farm Financial Crisis

A central proposition of the theory of uneven development is that capital flows at an uneven rate into various industries in capitalist societies. Reasons for the differential flow of capital are many: the relative cost of labor, demand for products, and changes in the industries that provide the inputs or market the products of a particular industry. Consequences of uneven rates of capital investment are varying levels of technological development, different wage rates, and uneven rates of growth.

Capital flows among industries can be studied at an aggregate level or through case studies; each approach has advantages and disadvantages. I have chosen to use a case study approach because it provides more detailed information on social, political, and economic causes and consequences of capital flows. In this chapter, I discuss uneven development in agricultural production and the role of finance capital in promoting the farm financial crisis of the 1980s. I am concerned primarily with identifying the factors contributing to the farm debt crisis and how capital flows influence the forms of production in agriculture. Uneven development in agriculture refers to "the maintenance of noncapitalist units of production within a larger capitalist social formation (Mann, 1984:413).

For decades, Marxists and non-Marxists have debated whether agricultural production resists capitalist penetration or follows the same path of capitalist development as other industries (Chayanov, 1966; Lenin, 1938). This issue first developed after the Russian revolution when the collectivization of the peasantry was considered. According to Lenin, agriculture should be

collectivized like all industries if socialism was to
develop. Chayanov, on the other hand, contended that
agricultural production was neither capitalistic nor
socialistic. As a result, the peasantry should not be
forced to follow along the same path as other
(capitalistic) industries.

There appears to be a growing consensus in the
literature on agricultural development that capitalism
does penetrate agricultural production, although in a
different form from other industries (Mooney, 1983).
Peculiar qualities of agricultural production may
contribute to this uneven nature of development (Mann and
Dickinson, 1978; Mann, 1984). Mann and Dickinson (1978)
argue that the gap between production time and labor time
in agricultural production is a critical deterrent to
capital. In addition, the amount of risk involved in
agricultural production discourages capitalists from
investing directly in this industry. As a result,
agriculture does not develop at the same rate, or
possibly even take the same path, of development as other
industries.

This does not mean, however, that capitalism is
unable to penetrate agricultural production. These
obstacles are not immutable. Capitalism takes hold of
agriculture in ways that hide the structural changes
occurring in production. In American agriculture, this
form of penetration often leaves observers with the
impression that families continue to manage, own, and
operate production units independent of outside influence
(Vogeler, 1981). This ideological position is important
in hiding capital intervention into agriculture. For
example, although poultry production in this country
continues to be dominated by family labor farms, most of
the management has been removed to processing firms who
require contracts of all producers. This structural
arrangement enables the processing firms to take less
risk in the production, yet it enables processors to
maintain their control of the markets.

Most contemporary debates concerning structural
change in agriculture focus on how surplus is extracted
from producers. In this chapter, I examine the various
debates regarding the applicability of Marx's theory of
value to agriculture. I argue that surplus value is
extracted from agriculture in a variety of forms. This
is relevant to our discussion of credit because one of
the most important forms of surplus value is interest.
Debt relations are not only a means of exploitation, but

also a basis for control and social change in agriculture. The farm financial situation of the 1980s has produced a crisis with the potential of fundamentally restructuring production. Finance capital may serve as the basis for the long-term change in the structure of agriculture in the United States. This process has been facilitated by state policies encouraging capital investment in agriculture. In many cases, farm policies promoting favorable conditions for family farms ultimately stimulate capital investment in these sectors. The result is a loss of family farms and the expansion of outside capital in agriculture.

AGRICULTURE AND SOCIAL CHANGE

There are a variety of theoretical positions in the literature on agricultural development in capitalist societies. One position is that the absence of wage labor in many realms of agricultural production precludes the application of Marx's value theory to agriculture (Friedmann, 1981). Because family labor farms exploit their own labor, rather than wage labor, producers are able to resist competitive pressures of the economy and will not necessarily evolve into large, corporate forms of organization (Nikolitch, 1965). Many of these analyses are extensions of Chayanov's theory of peasant economy. According to Chayanov, peasants do not maximize profits, but structure their decision making around the consumption needs of the family unit and minimizing the drudgery of labor. Following this logic, family labor farms would expand production as the consumption needs of the family increased. Therefore, production decisions reflect demographic changes occurring in the family unit.

An interesting variation of this position is Friedmann's (1980) analysis of how simple commodity producers were able to replace corporate farms in the Great Plains at the end of the 19th century. Theorists who take this position assume that agriculture may resist the same tendencies toward greater centralization and concentration that occur in other sectors of the economy. Uneven development in agriculture, according to these theorists, occurs because the different labor of family farms does not require producers to make a profit. As a result, agriculture inevitably lags behind other industries that are not based on family labor systems. According to these theorists, profits made by agribusiness firms, rent paid to landlords, and interest paid to banks do not represent surplus value, but are based on unequal exchange between simple commodity producers and capitalists. These relations will not lead to a necessary transformation of simple commodity production in agriculture.

A second group of theorists contend that agriculture develops according to the logic of capital; thus, wage labor will eventually replace family labor in agricultural production (de Janvry, 1980). Capital is highly concentrated and centralized in the input and output sectors of agriculture, and the production sector has become much more centralized over the past fifty years (Goss, Rodefeld, and Buttel, 1980). These theorists contend that Marx's theory of value can be applied to analyses of agriculture in a nonproblematic manner (Friedland, Barton, and Thomas, 1981). The cost/price squeeze resulting from the market power of agribusiness firms in the input and output sectors of agriculture contributes to changes in the structure of agricultural production. Agriculture, according to these theorists, is not qualitatively different from other industries; capital flows into those realms of agriculture that are most profitable. Eventually, capital will produce wage labor relations in all sectors of agriculture.

A third position in this debate is that surplus value is extracted from agricultural producers in alternative forms. Mooney (1983) argues that surplus value is drawn from agricultural producers through contract farming, debt relations, tenancy, and part-time employment off the farm. Mooney's analysis is based on an extension of Wright's (1978) work, which places most family labor farms in contradictory class locations. Contradictory class locations are outside traditional class positions (bourgeoisie, proletariat, and middle class); they have characteristics of more than one class. Mooney argues that agricultural production, however, is not inevitably moving toward capitalist forms of production (wage labor), instead capitalism takes a variety of detours in agriculture:

> much Marxian analysis contains, explicitly or implicitly, a teleology concerning the destruction of simple commodity production and the movement of these persons toward a polarized class structure where the capitalist class faces only the proletariat. The

development of the concept "contradictory class location" in Wright's class analysis constitutes a break from this tradition insofar as such locations are not merely transitional but have effects or perhaps even some degree of permanence in capitalist social formations (Mooney, 1983:576).

In the following, I adopt the third position regarding capitalist development of agriculture. I focus primarily on the manner in which indebtedness provides a means by which value can be extracted from agriculture producers. Contrary to Mooney's proposition about the permanence of these relations, I argue that the logic of debt relations tends to produce structural changes in agricultural production. Indebtedness spurs structural changes during periods of accumulation crises. Social and political conditions, however, mediate this relationship between indebtedness and industrial change.

Value, Indebtedness, and Structural Change

Among Marxists, the most prevalent view of indebtedness is that it contributes to the survival, rather than the demise, of simple commodity production. For example, Kautsky (1980) argues that indebtedness will not bring about a transformation in agricultural production:

> The indebtedness of the peasant, in this sense is not only not revolutionary, but it is conservative; it is not a factor which forces the transition from one mode of production to another, but one which preserves peasant production in its current state (p. 79).

Kautsky's reasoning behind this claim is that it is against the interest of lenders to bring about a structural change in agricultural production.

> With the profitability of agriculture declining as a result of world competition, and the current stagnation and incipient decline of prices, and rents, usury capital shows less and less interest in expropriating the indebted peasantry if the property is auctioned, it stands to lose not only its interest but a part of its capital too (p. 79).

Thus, Kautsky disagrees with most Marxist accounts of
capitalism and agriculture that predict a disappearance
of production based on family labor. Kautsky sees the
persistence of family labor as consistent with the
development of capitalism. Mooney makes much the same
argument about debt relations and the proletarianization
of commodity producers:

> The transformation of the simple commodity producers
> toward proletarianization via the debt relation
> remains incomplete without foreclosure. . . .
> Barriers to complete proletarianization appear to
> issue from both the economic advantages to the
> creditor in perpetually extracting interest as
> against acquisition of the land and the debtor's
> capacity to generate enough surplus value to pay
> against such interest (1983:573).

These theorists assume that lenders prefer to extract
surplus value from borrowers and that they will not
foreclose on borrowers. This position, however, ignores
the historical and social dimensions of accumulation.
First, this ahistorical view of indebtedness assumes that
the nature of indebtedness and its meaning for lenders
and borrowers is static. I argue that social conditions
of accumulation have changed lenders' position towards
foreclosing on delinquent loans. The debt crisis has
altered the relationship between lenders and borrowers.
In many cases, lenders have nothing to gain by providing
borrowers with additional time or credit to repay their
loans. For many operators, there is very little chance
that they would even be able to meet the interest
payments, much less the principal. Lenders are in a much
better position if they foreclose on the loan and lease
the land in the short-run. This means that the banks
will take some losses, but they tend to be much more
acceptable than the alternatives.

We find that the present farm crisis has many
similarities to the conditions of farmers during the
Depression. At that time, insurance companies and
financial institutions took control of large amounts of
farmland. Although the farmland was eventually returned
to family operators, the evidence suggests that it is
perfectly logical for commercial banks to foreclose on
borrowers under certain conditions.

Second, this position fails to consider the changing
relationship between lenders and borrower. Changes in

the organizational structure of financial markets have
led to a form of technocratic control (Green, 1985),
structuring the profit imperative in financial
organizations. In other words, the bureaucratization of
finance institutions has important implications for the
loan policies and performance of these firms. It most
likely leads to a formalization of the evaluation
process, which works against smaller borrowers. Branch
banks and banking affiliates will be less likely to carry
these problematic loans in the future. Thus, the
changing structure of capital markets is undermining the
traditional relationship between banks and farm
borrowers.

In addition, banking deregulation has probably
increased the stress on smaller, rural banks (Gajewski,
1986; Milkove et al., 1986). As a result, the
relationship between lenders and farm borrowers is based
increasingly on formal rationality. A recent study by
the Office of Technology Assessment (1986) summarized
these changes:

> The severe financial stress of a large proportion of
> farmers and the recent regulatory and competitive
> changes in financial markets have combined to change
> forever the financial framework of farming. . . .
> Moreover, given the concentration in the banking
> industry, decisions about extending credit will more
> likely be made at large, centralized banking
> headquarters far removed from a loan applicant's
> farm. Loan decisions will thus be less influenced by
> the considerations of neighborly goodwill that
> frequently shaded the decisions of the more local
> banks (p. 137).

These changes in the banking industry and the farm
financial crisis threaten to accelerate the structural
changes in agriculture that have been occurring over the
past fifty years. I argue that indebtedness plays an
important role in social change in agriculture at this
particularly conjuncture. The credit system has become
an important source of uneven development. The state has
played a contradictory role in this process; it has
provided access to small farm operators while at the same
time promoting indirectly capital investment in
agriculture.

CREDIT AND AGRICULTURAL PRODUCTION

Increased capitalization of agriculture has enlarged the capital requirements of modern agriculture and has made it more difficult for producers to meet their production costs with retained farm earnings.[1] In 1870, 65 percent of the inputs into agricultural production consisted of labor, and 17 percent capital. By 1970, labor accounted for 16 percent of the inputs, and capital 62 percent (Cochrane, 1979). The total amount of interest payments for nonreal estate loans has increased from $186 million to $94.8 billion since 1940 (see table 4-1). The total amount of interest payments received from farmers for real estate loans has increased from $243 million to $97.3 billion since 1940 (United States Department of Agriculture, 1986). Not only have farm interest payments (nonreal and real estate) increased in an absolute sense, they have increased as a proportion of total farm expenditures. The ratio of farm interest payments to total farm expenditures has increased from 4 to 14 percent. Among factor payments, interest charges have increased more than any other farm expense (United States Department of Agriculture, 1986).

Several factors have contributed to the increased capitalization of agricultural production. Among the major factors underlining capitalization have been technological development in production, commodity programs, and tax policies. Cochrane (1979) argues that American farmers have been on a technological treadmill over the past fifty years, forcing agricultural producers to seek external sources of capital. In addition, by reducing much of the risk in production agriculture, the state has encouraged farm operators to increase the scale of production and to employ new technologies.

Capitalization of agriculture increased most rapidly in the 1970s. Several factors contributed to the rapid increase in indebtedness in U.S. agriculture. The Russian wheat purchase in 1972 had a dramatic effect; the price of wheat doubled in a few months and the outlook for agriculture suddenly improved. Another incentive for farmers to borrow large amounts during the 1970s was the real interest rate. The real interest rate takes into consideration the allowable deductions for income tax purposes and inflation. For the largest farmers, the interest rate was negative from 1970 to 1981. The prime

TABLE 4-1.
Total Farm Debt (Real and Nonreal Estate in Millions
of Dollars), 1940-85.

Year	Real Estate	Nonreal Estate	Total Debt
1940	5,512	3,207	8,720
1945	4,065	2,923	6,987
1950	5,184	6,493	11,678
1955	7,750	9,210	16,960
1960	11,269	12,526	23,795
1965	18,921	18,306	37,228
1970	27,360	23,123	50,483
1975	45,161	40,057	85,218
1980	87,781	82,426	170,207
1985	97,300	94,798	192,048

Source: United States Department of Agriculture,
Economic Research Service. Economic Indicators of the
Farm Sector: Balance Sheet Statistics. Washington,
D.C.: Government Printing Office (1986).

rate (the rate paid by the bank's best customers) was lower than the inflation rate from 1973 to 1975. The improved outlook for agriculture and the ensuing borrowing spree contributed to the rapid inflation of land values. Farmland values increased more rapidly than inflation for the entire decade. The increased equity of U.S. farmers made agriculture a wise investment for lenders.

Conditions favoring capital investment in U.S. agricultural production changed abruptly in the 1980s. Overspeculation of farmland, high interest rates, low inflation rates, depressed commodity prices, and rapidly declining farmland values contributed to the financial stress and bankruptcy of many farmers. These conditions were exacerbated by a recession in the world economy and a dramatic increase in commodity production by Third World countries. These developments reduced the demand for agricultural commodities produced in the United States.

Increased capital requirements of agriculture, combined with declining farm land values and assets, have produced a debt crisis. Although almost all segments of the farm population have been affected by the credit crisis, some groups, such as young operators who entered farming during the 1970s, have been disproportionately hurt (Bultena et al., 1986). In a study of Iowa farmers, Bultena et al. (1986) report that 11 percent of the farmers had debt-to-asset ratios exceeding 70 percent, and 22 percent of the farmers had debt-to-asset ratios of 41 to 70 percent. Farmers with debt-to-asset ratios greater than 70 percent are considered to be in imminent financial danger, and those farmers with 40 to 70 percent are at a substantial financial risk. They found those persons having high debt-to-asset ratios to be younger, more educated, operating larger units, and having higher gross farm incomes (Bultena et al., 1986:11). The high debt loads many farmers carry threatens to eliminate as many as 30 percent of the farmers in some agricultural regions by 1992.

A recent study by the U.S. Department of Agriculture (1985) also suggests that large farms are more likely to be under stress during the 1980s crisis. Among those farms that are very highly leveraged (debt-to-asset ratios over 70 percent), a large percent is in the largest sales class was highest of the various sales classes.

The debt crisis in U.S. agriculture illustrates the double-edged nature of capitalist credit. On the one hand, credit is increasingly important for the reproduction of capitalist relations. Plentiful credit at cheap rates enabled farmers and ranchers during the 1970s to expand their operations. Farmers and ranchers unable to gain access to credit, or who had to pay a higher price for it, were at a competitive disadvantage. On the other hand, credit facilitates structural change in agriculture. Conditions favoring capital investment in agriculture attracted nonagricultural investors and encouraged farm operators to expand their operations. This situation contributed to the farm financial crisis of the 1980s which threatens to accelerate the changes in the structure of agriculture that we have been experiencing over the past fifty years.

INFLUENCES OF THE STATE ON THE ALLOCATION OF AGRICULTURE CREDIT

What was the role of the state in the farm financial crisis of the 1980s? Many analysts argue that the state promotes the trend toward fewer and larger farms (Vogeler, 1981). Tax policies and agricultural commodity programs have encouraged capital investment in agriculture. In many cases tax advantages and commodity programs were supported by farm organizations because they favored agricultural producers over others in the economy. These policies have an unintended consequence of encouraging rapid structural change in commodities receiving preferential treatment. Through tax credits for investments and policies reducing the amount of risk, the state provides incentives for outside capital to enter agriculture and for farms to increase the scale of production. Some commodity groups, such as almond growers, have recognized the contradictory effects of these policies and have worked to eliminate them.

The state also influences agricultural development through the provision of loans. State programs providing direct lending or guaranteed or insured loans generally have the same effect as other agricultural policies-- producing fewer and larger farms. The variety of programs providing credit in agriculture promoted the conditions that ultimately led to the farm crisis in the 1980s. Without ready access to relatively cheap credit, the rapid capitalization in agriculture during the 1970s would not have been possible.

Recent accounts of the growing crisis in the banking industry point to energy, real estate, and agricultural loans as the source of these problems (Business Week, 1985). For major U.S. banks experiencing financial difficulties in 1984, such as Continental Illinois, Crocker National, and First Chicago, agriculture and energy loans were the most troublesome. Many smaller, rural banks with concentrated loan portfolios in agriculture are particularly vulnerable. These conditions affect not only smaller banks, but also the larger banks that often lend to rural banks. For example, Continental Illinois National Bank and Trust had correspondent relations with 43 percent of the banks in Iowa when it experienced its near-failure (Business Week, 1985).

With the growing unwillingness of private lenders to take risks with agricultural loans, the state is under greater pressure to take on responsibility for credit. The state, however, does not usually become directly involved in providing credit (O'Connor, 1973). According to Harrington et al. (1983:21), "the federal government will play a smaller role in providing credit to farmers as a result of the reorientation of the Farmers Home Administration away from emergency lending and toward supervised lending to family farms." The reason most often given by the Reagan administration for this shift in the FmHA is the need to reduce expenses of this program. The administration's position that further moratoriums on foreclosures are irresponsible is supported by conservative farm organizations, such as the American Farm Bureau, and by the American Bankers Association.

The state also indirectly influences the allocation of agriculture credit in several ways. For example, commodity programs have reduced significantly the risk in agricultural production. This has led to an increase in the availability of farm credit. Proposals by the Reagan administration to eliminate many farm programs would decrease the availability of credit because more risk would be imposed on producers.

The U.S. state provides four types of agricultural credit assistance: (1) credit through government-sponsored agencies, (2) government-insured loan programs, (3) government-guaranteed loan programs, and (4) direct loans. Government-sponsored loans are administered

primarily through agencies that are privately financed
after initial capitalization by the government, such as
the Banks for Cooperatives, Federal Intermediate Credit
Bank, and the Federal Land Banks. Government-guaranteed
and insured loans are a promise made by the federal
government to pay all or part of the principal and
interest on farm loans in the event of default. The
major difference between insured and guaranteed loans is
that premiums on insured loans are paid by the borrower
to cover losses and expenses (Meekhof, 1984). Direct
loans are provided by the state, for example the Farmers
Home Administration (FmHA) and Commodity Credit
Corporation (CCC) loan programs. Agriculture is the
major recipient of direct state lending, accounting for
about 61 percent of the loan obligations (Meekhof, 1984).

Among these programs, there has been a shift away
from direct to guaranteed loans. Under the FmHA, the
percentage of farm loans has declined dramatically, while
the percentage of other loans (e.g., housing) has
increased significantly. From 1960 to 1975, the share of
farm loans declined by more than half (Meekhof, 1984).
It would appear that farmers are shifting to public
sources of credit, but not direct government loans.

In my previous discussion of the relationship between
the state and capital flows, I hypothesized that the U.S.
state would have little influence on the flow of capital
between industries. This analysis of agricultural credit
suggests that the state has not directly influenced the
capital flow in agriculture. Direct farm loans by the
state have been reduced. The state, however, has
indirectly influenced the flow of capital in several
ways, making agriculture a more attractive investment for
outside capital and reducing the risk of farm loans in
many cases. While these indirect methods of influencing
capital flows have been important, they are not as
successful as more direct influences by the state on
credit allocation.

CONSEQUENCES OF THE FARM CRISIS
FOR THE CREDIT SYSTEM

Nejezchleb (1986:12) indicates that a large
percentage of the nation's small banks are located in
regions where there are significant problems in the
agricultural and energy sectors. As Nejezchleb
concludes:

Most of the loan-quality problems encountered by
small, established banks over the past five years
appear to be related to sectoral problems in the
central and western areas of the country. In the
aggregate, increases in loan-loss provisions have
been, by far, the major factor in declining
profitability at these banks, while interest margins
have continued to hold up quite well (p. 19).

The farm crisis has produced problems for many
financial institutions dependent upon agriculture loans.
In 1984, 79 banks failed, the highest since 1938, when 81
banks failed. In 1985, 120 banks failed. In 1986, 138
banks failed. As of August 28, 1987, 120 banks had
failed in the United States (59 were in Texas and
Oklahoma). The 120 bank failures in 1987 accounted for
almost $3.4 billion in assets. The majority of these
bank failures (92/120), were in small banks (less than
$25 million in assets).
The number of bank failures is only one measure of
the severity of the problem. Almost 300 banks,
accounting for over $7.6 billion in deposits, are
considered to have severe problems. The problem banks
are concentrated in four states: Iowa, Minnesota,
Missouri, and South Dakota--with 56 percent of the $7.6
billion in deposits considered to be vulnerable. The
thrift industry is experiencing even greater difficulty.
A recent General Accounting Office study found that 461
thrift institutions have a negative net worth (their
liabilities exceed their assets), 830 other savings and
loan associations had a net worth of less than 3 percent
(the regulatory minimum). Thus, 43 percent of the three
thousand savings and loan institutions are either
insolvent or close to it (New York Times, 1986c).
A major problem for these financial institutions is
the number of delinquent and nonperforming loans. In
1985, past due and nonperforming farm production loans
accounted for 9.2 percent of all such loans outstanding
compared with 4.6 percent of all other loans (Board of
Governors of the Federal Reserve System, 1986). Put
another way, farm production loans made up 2.9 percent of
all loans, but were 5.7 percent of total delinquent loans
and 7.8 percent of nonperforming loans. The proportion
of agricultural banks with a large number of
nonperforming loans has doubled in the past year.
An important question to address is: What happens to
a financial institution when it closes? Of the 79 banks

that failed in 1984, deposit payoffs were made in only four cases. In twelve cases, deposits in the failed bank were transferred to another bank and in the remainder of the cases the loans were assumed or a merger was assisted by the Federal Deposit Insurance Corporation (FDIC). Of the 120 bank failures in 1985, only 23 percent were not assumed by an existing bank. Arrangements for takeover differ substantially among cases. Banks are generally unwilling to take on the bad loans that contributed to the downfall of the failed bank. Thus, many borrowers are affected by the shift in ownership. Sixty percent of the failed banks in 1985 merged with existing bank holding companies. Of the 68 failed agricultural banks (defined as having more than 17 percent of their total loans as agricultural loans) in 1985, 66 percent were merged with bank holding companies.

OWNERSHIP AND CONTROL OF FARMLAND

The conjuncture of the farm crisis and banking deregulation may have long-term consequences for the structure of agriculture. Credit has become a most significant input into agricultural production. Although several factors have contributed to the changing structure of agriculture, such as the development and adoption of new technologies, government programs and policies, overproduction, and economies of scale, all of these factors stem from the capitalization of agricultural production (Goss et al., 1980; Vogeler, 1981). Increased capitalization of production places greater importance on access to and cost of credit. Deregulation of banking indirectly influences the cost of and access to credit by restructuring local financial markets.

Aside from the changes in the number and size of farms, the farm crisis and banking deregulation may contribute to a structural change in control of agriculture. The Farmers Home Administration holds the deeds to 3,997 farms and 1.1 million acres and the Farm Credit System has acquired 4,939 farms worth about $1.2 billion (New York Times, 1986a). Estimates of bank holdings are about 400 thousand acres with a value of $350 million (New York Times, 1987c). Insurance companies, who have been major lenders in agriculture, hold the deeds to about 2000 U.S. farms (New York Times, 1986a). Insurers' inventories, valued at $1.5 billion, total at least 1.5 million acres (<u>New York Times</u>, 1987c). Prudential Insurance Company acquired Northern Agricultural Trust Services (who manage 800 thousand acres), Metropolitan Life Insurance Company purchased Farmer's National Company (managing four thousand properties worth more than $1 billion), and Mutual of New York has bought Duff Farm Management (Center for Rural Affairs, 1986). These developments do not signal a shift in control if the land returned to farmers.[2] Much of this land, however, is managed by management firms, while other land is sold to investors.

Acquisition of land by insurance companies has proceeded most rapidly in the Midwest, where the farm crisis has been most severe. In Iowa, the value of farms held by insurance companies rose from $49 million in 1985 to $111 million in 1986 (Sinclair, 1987). During the same year the value of farms owned by insurance companies doubled to $20.5 million in South Dakota; doubled in Nebraska to $64 million; increased in Wisconsin 119 percent to $16.6 million; and in Minnesota, the value of farms held by insurance companies rose from $43 million to $64 million (Sinclair, 1987).

Among insurers owning the most land are Prudential, Travelers, John Hancock, Metropolitan Life, and Aetna. Prudential holds about 920 thousand acres worth $1.8 billion; Travelers owns 890 thousand acres; John Hancock holds 590 thousand acres; Metropolitan Life owns 510 thousand acres; and Aetna holds 415 thousand acres (Sinclair, 1987).

A recent study of Iowa farmers who have quit farming for financial reasons provides some additional evidence for the proposition that financial institutions are increasingly taking control of land. Otto (1986) found that in 33 percent of the cases where farmers quit because of financial reasons, the land is being held by the lender. In many cases, reports Otto, the land is being rented back to the original operator. In an additional 10 percent of the cases, the operator reported still using or renting the land, which may be an indication that the lending institution may actually have retained control.

If land values and commodity prices increase in the near future, financial institutions may take a short-term view and reap quick profits by selling their land holdings back to operators. There are few potential buyers and dumping the land on the market would decrease further the net worth of borrowers. A longer-term view

is for financial institutions to maintain ownership of
the land, which would lead to a resurgence of various
forms of tenancy in agriculture in the future. If
financial capitalists believe agricultural land prices
will increase in the long-run, they may speculate despite
the low initial yields in investment (Munton, 1985).

CONCLUSIONS

Deregulation of banking and the farm crisis may have
important implications for the changing structure of U.S.
agriculture. Availability and cost of agricultural
credit will be influenced by the changing structure of
the banking industry and the prospects for investment in
agriculture. Increased competitiveness in the banking
industry and decreased profitability in agriculture will
make commercial banks take a more cautious approach to
agricultural loans, particularly loans to small farm
operators. These changes have resulted in a
disinvestment of agricultural production by outside
investors. This is occurring at the same time as the
state is attempting to push agriculture in a more free
market direction because of the high cost of maintaining
the farm program. The depressed market for farmland and
the increased number of farm foreclosures is placing an
increased amount of farmland in the hands of financial
institutions. I have raised questions concerning the
conventional wisdom that financial institutions have no
interest in acquiring farmland.

Mooney (1986) argues that there are alternating
tendencies toward tenancy and indebtedness in
agricultural production systems of advanced capitalist
societies. Both tenancy and indebtedness present
legitimation problems that result in political solutions.
For example, the increase in tenancy during the 1930s led
to the rise of the Southern Tenant Farmer's Union and,
ultimately to a set of New Deal farm policies easing
access to credit and encouraging land ownership (Grubbs,
1971). According to Mooney, easy access to cheap credit,
combined with a number of other factors, contributed to
the farm financial crisis in the 1980s. Following this
argument, we might expect a set of political solutions
encouraging leasing arrangements as a means of
restructuring debt. Already many bankers are advising
farm operators to become more involved in various leasing
arrangements. One arrangement is for outside investors

to purchase farm machinery and lease the equipment to
farm operators. Under this arrangement, farm management
firms put together a group of investors and find
operators interested in leasing the equipment. Investors
are able to take advantage of tax provisions that enable
them to deduct the capital depreciation of the equipment.
Farm management companies benefit from the commission
they charge for the leasing arrangement. Finally, farm
operators allegedly benefit because their fixed costs
have been reduced. Several other innovative leasing
arrangements are available. If these trends continue, we
may experience an increased rate of tenancy in
agricultural production. The emerging form of tenancy
may closely resemble sharecropping arrangements that were
prevalent in the South following the Civil War. In other
words, farm operators would own neither the land nor the
equipment (e.g., tractor, combine, trucks) required for
production. Such an relationship would reduce much of
the risk for farm operators, but would leave producers
with much less control over the production process.

The changing relationship between lenders and farm
operators is not only influencing the structure of
ownership, but also control of the remaining farm
operations. Through interviews with loan officers in
bank holding companies, I have found bankers to be making
decisions about the farm operation, such as whether to
use conservation practices or to buy new equipment
(Green, 1984). Bankers are also providing advice on what
crops to plant and on how much to spend on food
(Sorenson, 1982). In many cases bankers refuse to make a
loan to farmers interested in alternative agriculture.
Bankers seldom make these decisions on the basis of sound
research or estimates of profitability. Instead, bankers
define what is considered a legitimate economic activity
and will refuse to make loans for nontraditional
activities. For example, a banker may refuse to lend to
a farmer that wants to start growing strawberries because
no one else in the region has tried it. A study by Zey-
Ferrell and McIntosh (1986; 1987) also found that bankers
influenced the type and extent of technology adopted by
farmers.

This analysis has demonstrated the contradictory
nature of capitalist credit. On one hand, access to
credit has become an increasingly important resource for
producers. Producers with more access to credit will
have a structural advantage over those producers that
lack access to external sources of credit. Farmers who

did not have access to capital in the 1970s put themselves at risk because other producers were becoming more profitable by borrowing capital at a reasonable rate. On the other hand, increased dependency on external credit sources contributes to structural change in the social relations of production. The farm crisis has required the state to intervene increasingly in financial and agricultural markets. The result has been a rapid increase in the costs of administering commodity programs and a large subsidy to the Farm Credit System to allow it to continue.

NOTES

1. There is some evidence to suggest, however, that this trend in farm debt may have ended. A recent study by the Board of Governors of the Federal Reserve System (1986) suggests that unless conditions in the farm sector change dramatically in the next few years, it is likely the use of farm credit will decline in the future.

Recent declines in the farm debt may represent the beginning of a long-term adjustment to a lower level of indebtedness. It is logical to expect this adjustment to continue until the debt of individual borrowers is below the market value of their assets and their debt service requirements can be met from operating profits. Furthermore, historical experience also suggests that, once established, cautious attitudes toward use of credit may persist for some time after it has again become profitable for farmers to employ financial leverage (p. 12).

2. This situation, at the very least, suggests a rapid increase in the size of production units over the next few years.

5

Finance Capital
and Regional Development

Uneven development of spatial structures appears to
be an essential feature of capitalism. David Harvey's
(1973; 1982; 1985) innovative work has triggered an
interest in the link between spatial structure and social
structures and processes. Harvey argues that a theory of
capitalist space is essential to Marx's theory of
accumulation and that this aspect of the theory has been
ignored. Space is a commodity, having both a use value
and an exchange value. In capitalist societies, the
pursuit of use value and exchange value is often
contradictory and leads to conflict. The struggle over
the pursuit of these goals produces basic spatial
patterns. Logan and Molotch (1987:2) suggest that "in
light of this tension we can better understand the
political dynamics of cities and regions and discover how
inequalities in and between places--a stratification of
place as well as of individuals and groups--are
established and maintained." As Smith (1984) suggests,
uneven development is the systematic geographical
expression of the contradiction inherent in the very
constitution and structures of capital. This
contradiction involves the opposing tendencies between
differentiation and equalization. The need to study
capitalist space has been echoed by urban (Castells,
1977) and rural (Gilbert, 1982) sociologists.
    In this chapter, I link the spatial and social
processes of accumulation by focusing on the role of the
credit system in promoting uneven regional development.
My analytical focus is on the effects of finance capital
on development in the southern United States. The South
is a particularly interesting case study because
underdevelopment in the region has often been attributed

to lack of capital (James, 1978). For much of the 19th and 20th century, the South has been a net capital importer. The growth of the southern banking system spurred development in the region, but its structure makes that growth extremely precarious. The growing conflict between regional and national finance capital, and finance capital and industrial capital, will influence the nature of economic growth and development in the region. Banking deregulation is unleashing new economic forces that will influence regional capital flows in the United States. These changes in financial markets will exacerbate problems of uneven regional development and make it more difficult to develop policies to reduce these inequalities.

THE SOUTH AND CAPITAL FORMATION

The South and West were relatively slow to integrate into the national capital markets, as evidenced by different price structures and loan practices in these regions. Several explanations have been offered for this phenomenon. Sylla (1969) argues that the lack of integration was a result of the monopolistic power of the local banks in the South, particularly in rural areas. As a result, interest rates in the South remained significantly higher than the national average. James (1978) argues that the capital shortage in the South was because of the higher risk of cotton production and inadequate mechanisms for transferring capital between regions. The reduced importance of cotton production and the development of a means for the interregional transfer of capital eliminated any regional differences in the performance of commercial banks. After the Civil War, four methods of transferring capital between regions were developed. First, interbank loans became a popular means of transferring short-term funds between regions. Interbank loans were more prevalent in the South (almost 50 percent of the total loans). Correspondent relations are still quite prevalent among commercial banks in all regions.

A second method of transferring capital between regions is by direct interregional loans. Capital is transferred by a bank's loaning money to a borrower in another region. Wheeler and Brown (1980) point out that interregional loans occur in a structured pattern. Corporate links to banking services move hierarchically;

larger corporations are much more likely than smaller
ones to conduct their banking business with banks outside
the region. Obviously, this relationship is influenced
by the greater likelihood of large corporations to have
branch plants and for branch plants to obtain credit
outside of the region.

A third method of facilitating the transfer of
capital is interregional holding of bank stock. This
obviously occurs within the limits of interstate banking
regulations. James (1978) demonstrates the existence of
a pattern for greater absentee ownership in western and
southern banks. In many cases, this situation has
permitted eastern banks to expand their portfolios and
has often been the only form of investment of interest to
eastern banks.

The fourth method of transferring funds between
regions is the commercial paper market. As banks obtain
commercial paper, they are participating in a market that
facilitates the flow of capital from one region to
another. Davis (1963) argues that the development of a
commercial paper market was the major institutional
change leading to market integration of towns and cities
in the West and South. Commercial paper markets have
become the most important mechanism for local banks to
transfer capital out of a community.

Other researchers, most notably Genovese (1965),
argue that it was not institutional barriers, but the
manner in which credit was allocated in the South that
inhibited industrial development.

> The banking system of the South serves as an
> excellent illustration of an ostensibly capitalist
> institution that worked to augment the power of the
> planters and retard the development of the
> bourgeoisie. . . . In the West, as in the Northeast,
> banks and credit facilities promoted a vigorous
> economic expansion. During the period of loose
> Western banking (1830-1844) credit flowed liberally
> into industrial development as well as into land
> purchases and internal improvements . . . The
> slave states paid considerable attention to the
> development of a conservative, stable banking system,
> which could guarantee the movement of staple crops
> and the extension of credit to the planters.
> Southern banks were primarily designed to lend the
> planters money for outlays that were economically
> feasible, and socially acceptable in a slave society:

the movement of crops, the purchase of land and
slaves, and little else (p.21).

In sum, Genovese argues that it was the class
character of the banking system that directed capital
away from industrial expansion in the South. In the
West, manufacturers and merchants dominated the board of
directors of the region's banks. In the South, planters
controlled the board of directors and bank policies
reflected the interests of landowners. The conservative
character of landowners directed development in a
separate path from that taken in other U.S. regions.
This path of development maintained the slavery system
and restricted the development of wage labor, and
competition for labor, in the South.

Ransom and Sutch (1972) provide additional evidence
supporting Genovese's argument. They show that southern
merchants held monopoly power after the Civil War in
capital markets. Local merchants, who were also the
landowners in many cases, prevented production for local
consumption through debt peonage. At the center of these
analyses is an argument that the conservative nature of
development in the South was based in the control of
landowners and was facilitated by their influence over
financial institutions in the region. These institutions
prevented the type of development that would threaten the
hegemony of landowners. In the antebellum period, the
institutional structure of the credit system and the
class character of southern banks promoted a capital
shortage in the region.

After the Civil War, however, an institutional
structure was in place that facilitated capital flows
between regions. This fact raises an important question:
What were the factors contributing to the capital
shortage in the postwar South? As Billings (1979) and
Ransom and Sutch (1972) point out, the planter class
retained its power over capital markets after the Civil
War. Although the South began to industrialize after the
Depression, the development took on a qualitatively
different character from modernization in the North. The
South's industrial development was built on a low-wage,
low-skill work force and contributed to the persistent
gap in income and living conditions between North and
South (Hirschman and Blankenship, 1981). In addition,
conditions of the postwar economy in the postbellum South
discouraged capital investment in the region. Commercial

banks seeking to find low-risk investments drained
capital from the region.

SUNBELT DEVELOPMENT AND CREDIT

The rapid growth in the South over the past two
decades has been well documented in the popular press and
in academic articles (Sale, 1975; Watkins and Perry,
1977). Several factors have contributed to this growth:
low taxes, a "good business climate," the low cost of
labor, and state policy. Most neoclassical economic
accounts of this phenomenon suggest that migration to the
Sunbelt and the low cost of labor in the region were the
most significant factors contributing to this
development. This explanation assumes that capital flows
respond to, rather than cause, this development. In
other words, it was rational for financial institutions
to shift capital to the South because of the lower costs
of production in the region compared to the North.
Neoclassical economists assume that these processes will
work to produce a regional convergence in advanced
capitalist societies. The neoclassical account, however,
never raises the question: Why did the Sunbelt develop
when it did? To answer this question adequately we must
view regional development as a historical phenomenon. In
other words, we need to be able to explain why a certain
type of development occurs at a particular time.
Spatial specialization occurs because of the
obstacles capital faces in its drive to expand.[1]
Different historical conditions require different
strategies by the owners of capital. Regional
disparities change depending on the power of corporate
capital and the working class. For example, labor
victories in the northern United States increased the
cost of production, combined with the deskilling of the
production process, led capital to industrialize less
developed regions within the U.S. and abroad (Fox, 1978).
In this sense, southern development could be
characterized as that of a "favored colony" (Persky,
1973).
Previous analyses of southern development suggest
that the credit system played an instrumental role in
facilitating the conservative character of development in
the region. The class character of local banks (e.g.,
who sits on the board of directors) and the institutional
structure of the banking system (e.g., structural means

of facilitating the flow of capital) worked against the type of modernization occurring in the North at the time. The evidence suggests, however, that these factors were less important in the postbellum period. What explains the persistence of underdevelopment and flight of capital in the region? In the following, I suggest that the character of the credit system contributed to the capital drain in the South, and ultimately to its underdevelopment.

Spatial shifts in capital have important consequences for the social structure, resulting in a reformed capitalist space. Capital flows between regions mediate class conflict and are channeled to different regions through financial institutions. According to Glasberg's (1981; 1985; 1987) bank hegemony theory of control, financial institutions exert dominance over industries and firms by defining the options available for investment. For example, financial institutions may define certain areas or regions as unattractive for investments, which deters industrial development in that area (Ratcliff, 1980). Evaluation of the profitability of investing in a particular region may change because of unionization, increases in taxes, or growth in political activities within the working class or among minorities. On the other hand, when a region is considered an attractive investment by financial institutions a net inflow of capital is likely.

Financial institutions thus play an important, active role in regional development. Because financial institutions seek to invest in low-risk opportunities, they may ignore investments that in the long-run may be profitable and contribute to regional economic development. Shifts in the direction of capital flows between regions are only partially the result of factor costs (i.e., wages, costs of production, location of markets). Social and political factors play an important role in influencing the direction of capital flows in regions. For example, social unrest and the social organization of financial institutions and markets influence the level and manner in which capital is allocated in a region. Finally, historical factors shape decisions influencing the allocation of credit. From a neoclassical economic position, the lack of economic development in the South should have provided an important economic incentive for capital investment in the postwar period. Instead, the social conditions produced from plantation economies discouraged the type

of investment that would have improved the quality of
life in the region. It was only after the New Deal
programs and rural development policies in the 1960s that
the South began to experience significant improvements in
the social conditions that would attract capital into the
region.

In the following section, I analyze capital flows
between regions to assess the role of financial
institutions in promoting economic developing in the
South. I then examine the manner in which capital flowed
into the region. Following the neoclassical economists'
predictions we find that the capital drain in the South
has been virtually eliminated over the past few decades.
However, the shift in the flow of capital did not take
place until the U. S. economic crisis of the 1970s. This
suggests that social and political factors were a more
important determinant of the net flow of capital than
differential factor costs among regions. Second, I argue
that the type of development promoted by financial
institutions continues to place the southern economy in a
precarious position. Dependence on low-skill, low-wage
industries has proved to be devastating to many southern
communities in an era of increased global competition
from Third World countries. Moreover, it has produced
uneven development, between urban and rural areas, within
the South. Finally, deregulation will influence the flow
of capital among regions. By promoting a tighter link
between local and national capital markets, and
permitting interstate banking, the state may have created
the conditions for regional capital shortage in the
future. Banking deregulation has provided incentives for
southern banks to become more reliant on volatile
liabilities--uninsured deposits of more than $100,000 and
purchased funds--than banks in other parts of the U.S.
This may place southern banks in an increasingly
vulnerable position.

CAPITAL FLOWS AND THE SOUTH

To examine the role of finance capital in promoting
and facilitating development, I assess loans and deposits
in southern commercial banks. These data provide some
indication of the extent of capital formation and capital
flows among regions. Such data, however, can be
influenced by population size; under most circumstances,
a region with a large population will have more loans and

deposits than a less populated region. To control for
the effect of population size on the amount of loans and
deposits, I calculate the percentage of the total U.S.
population in each region and subtract this figure from
the regional share of loans or deposits in the region. A
positive figure indicates a larger proportion of loans or
deposits in the region than would exist if they were
distributed according to population size. A negative
figure points to a shortage in loans or deposits relative
to the size of the population. This measure for deposits
also considers differences in the level of wealth in
various regions.

The Northeast has the largest share of total
commercial loans in the country, both in absolute and
relative terms (table 5-1). Western banks have the
smallest total amount of commercial loans. Since 1970,
the Northeast has provided a larger share of commercial
loans than it would have if the loans were equally
distributed according to population; the South has a
smaller share of loans relative to its population. Both
the Midwest and the West have provided approximately the
same proportion of loans as population.

The dramatic decline in regional differences in loans
can be attributed to the rapid growth of southern banks
and a reduced growth rate in the largest money-center
banks in the Northeast. Asset growth in the largest
five southern banks grew six times faster than the five
largest U.S. banks between 1977 and 1987. The good
performance of the southern economy has contributed to
the loan growth in southern banks. However, an other
important factor is that southern banks have a much
smaller proportion of their portfolio in Third World and
energy loans. Thus, major regional banks such as
Wachovia and NCNB have continued to grow as banks with
large loans to Third World countries have experienced
reduced earnings and profits.

From 1970 to 1977, the absolute amount of banks loans
increased in all four regions. The Northeast led the
country with over $100 billion in loans, and the West was
lowest with a little over $50 billion in loans. The
percentage of total loans made by commercial banks in the
Northeast fell about 5 percent. During the same period,
the percentage of loans made by commercial banks in the
South increased 3 percent. Although the population in
the South increased dramatically during this period, the

TABLE 5-1.
Commercial Bank Loans (in billions of dollars) by
Region (1970, 1977, 1983)

	Region			
Loans	Northeast	Midwest	South	West
1970				
Loans	102.2	81.1	64.4	50.2
% Loans	34.3	27.2	21.6	16.9
% Loans Minus % Pop	10.2	- .6	-9.3	- .2
1977				
Loans	184.3	172.6	155.1	114.4
% Loans	29.4	27.6	24.8	18.3
% Loans Minus % Pop	6.6	.8	-7.5	.1
1983				
Loans	314.9	268.9	311.7	226.8
% Loans	28.1	23.9	27.8	20.2
% Loans Minus % Pop	6.9	-1.3	-6.2	.6

Source: U.S. Department of Commerce. State and
Metropolitan Area Data Book. Bureau of the Census,
Washington, D.C. (1979).

percentage of loans, relative to population increased in
the South and declined in the Northeast.

From 1977 to 1983, the Northeast stabilized in terms
of its percentage of loans relative to population; the
South continued to make gains. Regional differences in
the percentage of loans made by commercial banks
decreased over this period. Although these data suggest
that the South has made important gains in terms of its
share of U.S. loans, it still lags behind the Northeast
in terms of the relative percentage of loans made. The
data do show, however, that by 1983 the South's total
number of loans and percentage of loans is almost
comparable to that of the Northeast. Despite
improvements, commercial loans have not kept pace with
the population increase in the South, and continue to be
larger than the population size in the Northeast. This
suggests that relative to population size, the South has
not improved its position in terms of percentage of loans
made by commercial banks.

From the data in table 5-2 we can examine the
percentage of commercial bank deposits in the four U.S.
regions. In 1970, the Northeast had more deposits in
commercial banks than did the other regions. In both
absolute and relative terms, however, the Northeast has
been losing ground to the South. The Northeast's share
of total commercial deposits declined from 31.8 to 24.9
percent in 1983. On the other hand, the South's share of
total commercial deposits increased from 23.7 to 30.4
percent. This suggests that differences in the
performance of banks might be because of factors other
than the amount of deposits in these institutions.

By 1983, the South had the largest amount of deposits
in commercial banks among the four regions. The
Northeast continued to have a larger proportion of the
country's bank deposits, relative to its population.
However, the differences between the Northeast and the
South have declined considerably over this period.

In both relative and absolute terms, the South's
deficit in capital is disappearing. These data indicate
that there has been a greater convergence of deposits
than loans between 1970 and 1983. The rapid growth in
employment and population obviously fueled the flow of
capital into the South. The growth in deposits has
enhanced the economic position of many regional banks in
the South. Several of these regional banks may now be

TABLE 5-2.
Commercial Bank Deposits (in billions of dollars) by
Region (1970, 1977, 1983)

		Region		
Loans	Northeast	Midwest	South	West
1970				
Deposits	153.3	136.7	114.1	77.7
% Deposits	31.8	28.4	23.7	16.1
% Deposits Minus % Pop	7.7	.6	-7.2	-1.0
1977				
Deposits	267.8	261.2	247.3	163.2
% Deposits	28.5	27.8	26.3	17.4
% Deposits Minus % Pop	5.7	1.0	-6.0	- .8
1983				
Deposits	381.6	393.9	463.9	287.8
% Deposits	24.9	25.8	30.4	18.8
% Deposits Minus % Pop	3.7	.6	-3.6	- .8

Source: U.S. Department of Commerce. State and
Metropolitan Area Data Book. Bureau of the Census,
Washington, D.C. (1979).

considered as real competition to the money-center banks in the North. But the lag in loans suggests that southern banks continue to be conservative. A portion of the gap in loans between the Northeast and the South could be attributed to the fact that much of the growth and development in the South has occurred through branch plants locating in the region (Rosenfeld, Bergman, and Rubin, 1985). Branch plants typically do not obtain financing on their own. Financing is arranged by the headquarters or home office, often located in a Northern city. Thus, much of the growth of the Sunbelt may have been financed by northern, rather than southern, banks.

Many accounts of the rise of the Sunbelt attribute it to the increase in wages because of unionization in the North (Watkins and Perry, 1977). Below I examine the impact of some of these factors on the flow of capital into the South. This analysis will enable us to assess some of the propositions made by neoclassical and radical theorists concerning the factors influencing the flow of capital.

To analyze regional capital flows further, I perform regression analysis of the effects of a set of independent variables on total employment in 1982 using states as my units (table 5-3). The regression analysis includes a lagged variable for total employment (1967) and the total amount of commercial loans in 1982. Both of these variables should be positively related to employment.

In addition, I examine the effects of a variety of other factors influencing employment growth--weekly earnings, number of work stoppages, and per capita federal expenditures and taxes. We would expect weekly earnings, number of work stoppages, and federal taxes to be negatively related to total employment. Federal expenditures should be positively related to total employment. These variables were included as control variables in the analysis of the effect of loans on employment growth.

Total employment in 1967 is the best predictor among the independent variables of employment in 1982. The only other independent variable with a statistically significant effect on employment is total commercial loans. Surprisingly, none of the other variables are statistically related to employment. This finding indicates that performance of the banking system is a

TABLE 5-3.

Regression Analysis of Total Employment (1982) on
Selected Independent Variables

Independent Variables	b^a	Total employment $Beta^b$	S.E.b	Sig.
Employment (1967)	.615	.819	.036	.000
Loans (1982)	.006	.187	.002	.000
Weekly earnings (1979)	32.087	.023	163.268	.423
Work stoppages (1979)	.038	.007	.151	.801
Federal expenditures per capita (1979)	.002	.028	.002	.340
Federal taxes per capita (1979)	.005	.008	.018	.804
Constant	-76.250			
R^2	.968			
F	220.064			

a. Unstandardized regression coefficient.
b. Standardized regression coefficient.
Source: U.S. Department of Commerce. State and
Metropolitan Area Data Book. Washington, D.C., (1979)
and U.S. Department of Commerce. County and City Data
Book. Washington, D.C., (1982).

much better predictor of employment growth over the period than social and economic variables. Although the analysis does not provide conclusive evidence on the performance of banks, it does suggest that bank loans tend to have an independent effect on employment growth. Bankers are not perfectly rational actors who respond to the different economic conditions of regions and direct capital into those regions with the greatest profit potential. Instead, a number of other social and political factors influence the bankers' allocation of credit. As a result, credit is frequently allocated in an inefficient and inequitable manner.

BANKING STRUCTURE AND REGIONAL CAPITAL FLOWS

Economists concerned with the role of the banking system focus primarily on obstacles to the efficient flow of capital. Of primary concern to neoclassical economists is the relationship between the structure of the commercial banking industry and bank performance. There is a large body of research examining the consequences of branch banking systems and multibank holding companies for the performance of commercial banks. These researchers are critical of local monopolistic markets and often suggest that multiunit forms of banking provide more competition to the local market. It is necessary, however, to consider the structure of the national banking system and its effect on local capital markets.

I have discussed the mechanisms developed to facilitate the flow of capital between regions (e.g., interbank loans, interregional loans, interregional holding of bank stock, and the commercial paper market). One result of these mechanisms is the development of a hierarchical system of lending and borrowing. Rural banks and large borrowers in rural areas tend to borrow from urban areas. Similarly banks and large companies in smaller cities tend to borrow from banks in larger metropolitan areas (Wheeler and Brown, 1980). Noyelle and Stanback (1984) find that the largest 200 banks in the United States tend to be located in the North and that there has been little, if any, shift in the location of the parent office of these banks. As a result, much of the development in the South is financed by the largest banks in the North.

On the surface, this would appear to be a quite

favorable situation. Growth in employment, regardless of
the source of banking capital, would contribute to
regional economic growth and development. The type of
growth and development promoted by northern banking
capital, however, is extremely precarious. Much of the
South's growth, particularly in rural areas, has been
based on low-skilled, low-wage labor (Rosenfeld, Bergman,
and Rubin, 1985). This growth has slowed considerably in
recent years as competition by Third World countries has
taken many of these jobs. The result has been the
deindustrialization of many of the businesses that have
served as the South's industrial base. The textile and
apparel industries have been particularly hurt by
overseas competition. More than 750 thousand jobs have
been lost in the textile industry over the past ten
years. To remain competitive, textile producers must
mechanize their production process, which means a
continued loss of jobs.

The structure for financing industrial development in
the South has also contributed to a pattern of uneven
development. Although several regions in the South have
experienced rapid growth in recent years (e.g., Atlanta,
Raleigh-Durham, Dallas), other regions of the South are
beginning to lose population and employment once again.
Although many of these regions experienced some growth
during the rural renaissance of the 1970s, the recession
of the early 1980s put an end to that prosperity. The
Black Belt of the South continues to be ignored by
developers and bankers.

Finally, financing of local development projects from
banks outside the region continues the historical pattern
of draining profits from one region to support
development in another region. In other words, external
financing for economic development withdraws many of the
benefits for local economic development in the region.
Profits made from loans could be reinvested in local
economic development projects if interest payments
remained in local financial institutions.

This discussion suggests that the source of financing
is an important factor influencing the rate and character
of development. Local and regional banks tend to be more
concerned about the long-term growth of local economies
in the region. In the following, I discuss the differing
role of money-center and regional banks.

Money-Center versus Regional Banks

The conflict between regional and national finance capitalists will influence future development in the South. If the money-center banks are successful in entering these markets, the old system of northern banks providing most of the capital for southern development will return. If regional banks are successful in turning back the money-center banks, it could portend a new role for finance capital in the South. The outcome of this struggle will depend on action taken at the federal, state, and community level.

In the past, large money-center banks have displayed little interest in owning and controlling banks in other regions. The growing market in the South and the poor quality of loans in the Third World have spurred the interests of national banks in the region. Deregulation of banking has enabled large banks to gain a toehold in new markets. Some of this interest may be a defensive reaction to the entrance of nonfinancial corporations, such as Sears, into financial markets. If Sears is successful in establishing banking offices in all of its stores, a de facto interstate banking systems will exist, which may threaten the hegemony of the money-center banks.

In response to these developments, regional banks have attempted to protect their markets. First, regional banks have expanded geographically. Growth has occurred through the bank holding company form of organization and the branch banking system. The spark to merger mania in the banking industry was the Supreme Court's decision in June 1985 that interstate banking was constitutional. Between June 1985 and May 1987, banks in eight Southeastern states and the District of Columbia were involved in mergers and acquisitions worth more than $55.7 billion in commercial bank assets. "One out of every five dollars deposited in the Southeast is controlled by a bank in another state" (Schlesinger, 1987:33). As Schlesinger indicates

Thus interstate banking has apparently produced much of what its proponents in the banking community wanted: the opportunity to get bought out at hugely lucrative premiums; protection from takeovers by the community center banks of New York and California; shortcuts to portfolio diversification; and, most important (despite billowing clouds of sectionalist

rhetoric), access to retail deposits as a relatively
cheap, stable substitute for hot money that
increasingly funded big bank's assets (p. 33).

Second, regional banking pacts with reciprocal
relations have been successful in enabling regional banks
to growth without the threat of money-center banks
entering their markets. Such pacts permit banks in one
state to purchase banks in another state if the reverse
is also true. Regional arrangements such as this now
exist in the Southeast, Northeast, and Midwest. Banks
headquartered in three states--North Carolina, Georgia,
and Virginia--have benefited most from these pacts and
have been very aggressive in the southern markets.
Deposits gained through acquisition of out-of-state banks
by North Carolina banks are two-thirds of the deposits
within the state (Schlesinger, 1987). On the other hand,
there is not outside control of commercial banks in North
Carolina.

Third, regional banks have been successful in
pressuring state legislatures to pass laws keeping out
banks from specific states, such as New York. This issue
was raised as Citibank attempted to enter the southern
market. The U.S. Supreme Court affirmed the right of
states to pass such laws.

One reason for the increased strength of regional
banks is that they are located in high-growth areas where
bank deposits have increased more than 11 percent each
year since 1980 (Business Week, 1986a). This growth has
enhanced the market value of the stock of many regional
banks to the extent that a few regional banks are in a
position possibly to take over one of the money-center
banks. For example, the stock value of First Wachovia
and First Union, both in North Carolina, exceeds the
stock value of much larger banks, such as Manufacturers
Hanover and Mellon Bank. These regional banks have grown
at an extremely fast pace over the past decade. First
Union of Charlotte is one of the fastest growing banks in
the region. Over the past two years, First Union has
acquired 17 banks, more than tripling its assets to $26.8
billion (Business Week, 1987).

Another reason for the shift in power has been the
large number of troubled loans on the books of the
money-center banks; this has lowered the debt ratings of
these banks, making it more profitable for many large
corporations to go directly to the market and issue
commercial paper. If this trend continues, money-center

banks will move increasingly away from traditional bank
loans to other areas, such as overseas investment
banking. Such a scenario would mean that the regional
banks would become the real source of stability in the
U.S. banking system (Business Week, 1986a).

The success of the regional banks depends on their
ability to avoid major management problems resulting from
their expansion and acquisitions and the continued growth
of these regions. As the regional banks grow, they may
expand into areas where they have little expertise.
Regional banks face an interesting dilemma. They are
forced to expand to protect their existing market. As
they expand, however, they become less of a regional
bank, and look more like a money-center bank. Such a
strategy may backfire, as regulators may no longer see
any difference between the two types of banks.

CONCLUSIONS

Institutional mechanisms have integrated more tightly
southern banks into national capital markets. This
analysis suggests that financial institutions are
critical in actively directing capital flows among
regions. Shifts in the direction of capital flows are
not only due to factors costs of production, but also
social and political influences. For example, state
policies have facilitated the flow of capital into the
South over the past few decades. Thus, southerners are
told that future growth in their community depends on
maintaining a "growth ethic" and a continued willingness
to make concessions to businesses in order to attract
them to their community.

The flow of capital into the South has strengthened
regional financial institutions to the point that capital
is no longer being drained from the region to the same
extent that it has in the past. This has important
implications for future development in the region.
Although the entire banking industry has experienced a
decline in returns on assets from 1983 to 1986 (a decline
of almost 28 percent among all U.S. banks), the decline
was considerably smaller in the Southeast (almost 11
percent). Similarly, the capital to assets ratio
increased from 1983 to 1986 in southeastern banks by
almost 3 percent and increased less than 1 percent for
all U.S. banks.

The distinction between national and regional finance capitalists is an important one. Domhoff (1983) argues that local and national elites have much in common, but are frequently motivated by different interests. Local elites are concerned primarily with enhancing the growth of their particular locality (Logan and Molotch, 1987). National elites are driven to maximize profits, regardless of location decisions. These different interests are manifested only under certain conditions. The economic crisis in the 1970s and the necessity for large, money-center banks to seek new markets has contributed to this conflict. Regional banks will generally be much more interested in enhancing the long-term growth and development of the region than money-center banks.[2] Although both types of financial institutions are interested in maximizing profits, profits in regional banks are based primarily on development in the region.

Bank regulations have benefited regional and national finance capitalists. Deregulation and the entrance of nonfinancial institutions into financial markets, however, forces the money-center banks into markets previously dominated by regional banks. These developments can be interpreted as an attempt by industrial capitalists to reestablish the hegemony they had before World War II. Regional banks have been somewhat protected over the past decade. Increased deregulation and encouragement of the development of "superbanks," however, would undermine that protection. The result of these conflicts will determine whether the sun will continue to shine on the Sunbelt.

NOTES

1. See Markusen's (1985) interesting discussion of the relationship between industrial concentration, regional development, and specialization.

2. This is not to suggest that regional banks will be interested in local economic development. My own research suggests that in large bank holding companies and branch banks, decisions regarding loan applications are made increasingly in urban centers, rather than local

communities. This has important consequences for the allocation of credit. The growing number of mergers among regional banks in the South will exacerbate this problem.

6

The Debt Crisis
in the Third World

Debt crises have become commonplace in the 1980s. The debt crisis in the Third World first became public in 1982, when Mexico threatened to default on its loans to several U.S. money-center banks. Since that time, several countries (and U.S. banks) have been on the brink of disaster. Although no country has defaulted on its loans, a few countries, such as Peru, have stated they will limit repayment to a percentage of its Gross National Product.[1] The World Bank has imposed austerity programs on many Third World countries in an effort to improve their ability to repay loans. Although the situation has eased somewhat, Brazil's announcement in the spring of 1987 that it could not meet its loan payments created renewed concern over the stability of the world financial system.

In this chapter I look at some of the causes and consequences of the debt crisis in the Third World. Many analysts of the world debt crisis have argued that the rapid increase in oil prices was a major factor contributing to the spiraling debt of Third World countries. These analyses ignore, however, that many of the countries with the most severe debt problems were oil exporters. In addition, the debt crisis emerged at a time when oil prices were increasing. Rather than tying the world debt crisis to a particular event, I develop a structural analysis of the crisis and argue that it was a consequence of the financial system's tendency to produce instability in capitalist economies. In the late 1970s, commercial banks increased rapidly their investments in Third World countries and structured these loans to place the burden of risk on the borrowers. I begin with Minsky's (1980) hypothesis regarding the role of the

financial system in promoting economic instability.
Next, I examine some of the factors injecting instability
in the world market. These factors make it increasingly
difficult for individual nation-states to influence
capital flows on an international level.

THE MINSKY HYPOTHESIS

The Third World debt crisis stems from the
instability of the financial system. Neoclassical
economists assume that the economic system is basically
stable, and that the monetary system adjusts to demand.
Minsky (1982) argues, however, that the monetary system
has a propensity for disaster. In his interpretation of
Keynesian theory, Minsky contends that the economic
system is inherently unstable. Below, I describe the
process by which the monetary system contributes to the
destabilization of the economy. Following Minsky's
position, it will be argued that financial systems are
the source of instability in capitalism and tend to
promote speculation and rapid changes in capital flows.
Minsky argues that debt crises begin with a shock to
the macroeconomic system, a displacement. Examples of
these outside shocks have been the outbreak or end of
war, a bumper harvest or crop failure, and widespread
adoption of an invention. One consequence of the outside
shock is that profit opportunities change in at least one
sector of the economy. New profit opportunities create
objects of speculation. Historically, objects of
speculation have been agricultural land, commodities
(e.g., copper or gold), or new industries. Profit
opportunities lead to a boom fueled by the expansion of
credit and an enlargement of the money supply. Credit is
expanded not only by increasing the means of payment, but
also by developing new credit instruments, forming new
banks, and expanding credit outside of banks.
A speculative boom attracts a large number of firms
and households that are not normally involved in these
activities. Therefore, speculative booms lead away from
normal, rational behavior, and develop into "bubbles" or
"manias." As this process develops further, interest
rates, velocity of circulation, and prices all continue
to increase (Kindleberger, 1978:18-19). Interest rates
increase because the demand for credit is driven up by
the attractive investment opportunities. Money capital
is circulated more rapidly through finance institutions

because of the good investment opportunities in these speculative activities.

Eventually, prices peak and begin to fall and speculators realize that the market will not go any higher. Kindleberger (1978:19) refers to this stage as "revulsion." At this stage, financial institutions no longer invest in these activities. Bankers decide that further investment in these areas would be risky. A panic develops at this stage and continues until prices fall so low that new investors move in or trade is cut.

Although Minsky challenges many of the Keynesian assumptions about the stability of capitalism, he concludes that a return to rational behavior will produce market equilibrium. Either the bubble will burst, returning investors to a rational state, or a lender-of-last-resort will intervene. Although structural changes in the financial system are necessary to prevent speculative booms from undermining the economy, Minsky believes the structure is basically sound, needing only minor repairs.

Minsky's analysis of debt crises is an improvement over most neoclassical and Keynesian analyses of credit, however, because it adds a dynamic element to market processes. In other words, Minsky does not attribute instability to external factors, such as government intervention or market imperfections, but he believes that instability is built into capitalism. A major source of that instability is the financial system. Minsky, however, does not take his analysis to its logical conclusions. An analysis of the financial system needs to locate this activity in the larger political economy. For example, what are the social and political factors influencing the direction of capital flows and how might these factors affect the ability of capital markets to return to stability. In addition, his analysis ignores the transnational character of capital, which makes it increasingly difficult for a lender-of-last-resort to restore stability to the market.

Marx's theory of finance capital enables us to examine the finance system as a source of social transformation in capitalism. Credit performs a specific social function in capitalist society, forming the basis of exchange by linking producers to the market (Brett, 1983). In Marx's analysis, debt crises are inherent in the logic of capitalist credit. Financial systems-- through their unique ability to create money capital-- tend to produce conditions favoring overproduction.

These tendencies, however, are exacerbated by the rise of transnational banks and financial institutions. Transnational capital makes it increasingly difficult for states to influence through traditional means the flow of capital. Because of these developments, it becomes increasingly difficult for lenders-of-last-resort to provide stability to the economic system.

What is the role of the financial system in promoting the Third World debt crisis? I argue that the poor quality of domestic loans, banking regulations, and the large supply of capital in the Euromarket shifted dramatically the flow of capital to overseas markets. A consequence of these developments is that the United States is unable to influence the direction of capital flows to the extent it once did. A world recession, produced by the monetarist policies of developed capitalist societies, plunged Third World countries into a debt crisis. To maintain their access to credit, Third World countries are forced to meet the austerity conditions of the International Monetary Fund (IMF). Rather than returning the system to stability, these developments have pushed the world financial system further into a crisis situation.

EMERGENCE OF THE CRISIS

A prevalent explanation for the Third World debt crisis is that the oil crisis of the early 1970s increased the debt of the developing countries. Petrodollars were recycled from the Organization of Petroleum Exporting Countries (OPEC), through the European branches of transnational banks, to the developing countries. According to this view, the spiraling cost of oil fueled the rate of inflation and created a trade deficit in the impoverished developing countries that were not oil exporters. It should follow, then, that lower prices of oil should have relieved the debt crisis in the Third World countries. This did not happen.

The rise of the Euromarket has important implications for the debt crisis in the Third World. Versluysen (1981) traces the birth of the Euromarket to 1957. Three factors contributed to the rise of the Euromarket. First, the tension of the Cold War led the Soviet Union and East European countries to move their deposits out of the United States, which spawned an offshore currency deposit market. Second, institutional factors, such as Regulation Q and restrictions on capital movement, provided an incentive for U.S. corporations to seek offshore financing. To maintain their profits, U.S. banks followed their corporate customers to overseas markets. Third, the U.S. balance-of-payment deficit produced additional international liquidity.

An assumption many analysts made of the debt crisis is that money-center banks sought to maximize their profits by making loans with relatively high interest rates to countries that would under normal circumstances not have received loans. In fact, several factors influenced banks' risk assessment during this period, which made the loans seem quite reasonable at the time. These loans were quite rational for individual bankers, but irrational for the financial system. Most developing countries were producing raw materials for the world market and the prices for these commodities skyrocketed in the mid 1970s. Real interest rates were close to zero, and during a few periods were even negative. Developing countries were willing to pay more for loans than were the domestic customers of commercial banks. Banks could earn a higher rate of return by lending to the developing countries because the margins and service fees were higher on the loans to the developing countries (Aronson, 1977). Because the loans were made to governments rather than private investors, the banks regarded the borrowers as immune from bankruptcy. Finally, the World Bank was considered a lender-of-last-resort for the developing countries.

In addition to the increased availability and demand for credit, structural changes in lending exacerbated the flow of capital into the developing countries. First, OPEC countries deposited their money in European branches of U.S. and European banks (Watkins, 1986).[2] Because reserve requirements in the U.S. are relatively high, banks were able to lend out more money than would have been possible if the funds were deposited in the United States. Second, OPEC countries insisted on making only short-term deposits. In response, commercial banks adopted floating loan rates and financed long-term loans to developing countries. Although this practice generated a guaranteed profit, it also placed most of the risk on the developing countries. Finally, because of the size of the loans the developing countries requested, the money-center banks persuaded regional banks to put up some of the capital for "jumbo" loans (Watkins, 1986).

This practice spread the risk of loans to Third World
countries throughout the U.S. banking system. Thus, the
changing structure of international capital markets and
the structure of Third World loans made most of these
investments quite logical from the bankers' standpoint.

Wood (1986) argues that it was also logical for
developing countries to borrow as much as they did. The
rapid increase in the price of oil created financial
needs that could not be met with aid alone. A relatively
high rate of inflation meant that real interest rates
were extremely low. A final consideration for developing
countries was that private lending became a means of
avoiding the discipline of institutions administering
aid.

> Euromarket loans in the 1970s usually differed from
> aid in both of these respects, linked at most only
> vaguely to specific projects and carrying few
> explicit conditions apart from those dealing with
> repayment and potential default (Wood, 1986:245).

The events of the 1970s radically changed the social
definitions of credit worthiness and risk. In many
instances, credit worthiness was assessed by how much
debt a country could obtain rather than by its ability to
repay the loans. Banks were no longer making loans based
on the feasibility of a project, but on the economic
prospects of the developing countries, which were
generally good in the 1970s. Thus, a loan for a specific
project that would not be considered a good risk in the
past would be granted because the banks were considering
the country's total risk situation. Even evaluating the
total indebtedness of a country, however, was difficult
because banks could not control the country's ability to
borrow more funds from other banks.

The increased availability of and demand for credit,
and the changing lending patterns and risk assessments of
banks, expanded the supply of credit to developing
countries. The flow of capital into the Third World,
however, was not even. Although new criteria were being
used to assess the risk in these new loans, other
noneconomic criteria were equally important. Dewitt and
Petras (1979) argue that bank capital has been channeled
into regimes with certain characteristics. Generally,
regimes that have received loans tend to be committed to
foreign flows of capital, promote easy access to raw
materials, have large internal markets, and have

substantial surplus labor pools. Thus, access to credit was used as a means of rewarding regimes that were favorable to the United States and multinational corporations.

Probably the most significant factor determining whether countries are recipients of bank capital is whether they have signed an IMF agreement. Korner et al. (1986) indicate:

> Many governments of developing countries reluctantly decide to sign IMF agreements because this is the only method of restoring the country's creditworthiness on international capital markets. If balance-of-payments and budget deficits have reached such levels that creditors are alarmed about the repayment of their loans, governments have no choice but to negotiate a stabilisation programme with the 'faceless men' of the IMF. Such are the rules of the international finance system. Even today the actual amount of the loan is of secondary importance; the decisive factor is the 'seal of approval' which an IMF agreement gives to the government's economic policy (pp. 53-54).

The stabilization programs of the IMF primarily focus on the extent to which the local economy is structured for export. The IMF typically requires government reduction of the budget deficit, devaluation of local currency, restrictions on domestic credit, and cuts in subsidies for public goods. Goals of these programs are to enhance the permeability of Third World economies and increase demand for exports.

U.S. banks have about $130 billion in loans to developing countries (Watkins, 1986). This means that for every percentage point in interest not paid, banks lose about $1.3 billion. The majority ($86 billion) of these loans have been made to Latin American countries. In table 6-1, I present data on the amount of debt among developing countries with the largest debt from 1974 to 1983.

As the debt in Third World countries mounted, the price of basic commodities exported plummeted. From the late 1970s to the early 1980s, the value of commodity exports fell dramatically for sugar, cocoa, and cotton

TABLE 6-1.
Developing Nations with the Largest Debts (1974-83)

Country	External Debt in millions of dollars	
	1974	1983
Mexico	8181.2	66731.6
Brazil	11004.8	58068.1
Argentina	3247.3	24592.6
Indonesia	6358.2	21768.8
Korea	4365.9	21472.4
India	11471.4	21276.6
Egypt	2850.9	15530.8
Turkey	3123.7	15396.3
Algeria	3304.7	12915.6
Venezuela	1493.0	12911.4
Nigeria	1219.7	11757.2
Malaysia	866.6	10665.2
Philippines	1054.1	10385.4

Source: United Nations, Statistical Yearbook 1983/1984. New York (1986). For further details see World Debt Tables, 1984-1985 edition published by The World Bank, Washington, D.C.

(see table 6-2). The world economy experienced a deep recession during this period, created by the monetary policies of the developed nations. Decreased demand for basic commodities led to loss of revenues and eventually to an inability by Third World countries to repay their loans.

In sum, two major factors contributed to the spiraling debt of Third World countries. First, the rapid price increase of oil enlarged the availability of capital for investments. Large commercial banks in Europe and the United States sought new profitable outlets for capital. The performance of the developing economies made Third World countries an attractive investment. In addition, the stagnating economies of developed societies made aid to Third World countries an unlikely prospect. Although the oil shock of 1973 contributed to the debt crisis, it was not a precipitating factor. Lomax (1986) suggests that the second oil shock (1979-80) had a much more significant impact on the debt situation then the 1973 oil crisis. Following the second oil shock, nominal and real interest rates grew more rapidly, OECD countries generated a recession and adopted more protectionist policies. A result of these policies was a fall in world trade which made it impossible for Third World countries to repay the debts they had incurred during the previous decade. The big banks' response was to increase substantially the level of lending to Third World countries.

Korner et al. (1986) add that accounts of the debt crisis pointing to OPEC oil policies as the cause ignore the timing of financial problems in the Third World. They suggest that:

> it is paradoxical that it was in 1982, the year in which oil prices showed a clear downward tendency for the first time in ten years, that the debt crisis crashed over debtor and creditors. And it was the oil exporting countries, such as Mexico, Venezuela, and Nigeria who were hit the hardest (p. 27).

The second precipitating factor to the international debt crisis was the adoption of monetarist economic policies in the United States and several European countries and the decline in basic commodity exports in

TABLE 6-2.
Latin American Primary Commodity Exports Market
Prices, 1973-82.

Commodity	1973	1980	1982
Maize			
($/metric ton)	100.8	125.0	109.2
Percent change		24.0	-13.4
Bananas			
(cents/kilogram)	28.7	37.4	37.4
Percent change		30.3	0.0
Sugar			
(cents/kilogram)	17.3	63.2	18.6
Percent change		65.3	-71.5
Coffee			
(cents/kg)			
Brazil	364.4	458.3	318.9
Percent change		25.8	-30.4
Colombia	408.8	383.7	327.6
Percent change		-6.1	-14.6
Cocoa			
(cents/kilogram)	340.2	260.4	173.6
Percent change		-23.5	-33.3
Soybeans			
($/metric ton)	268.3	296.3	244.6
Percent change		10.4	-17.5
Cotton			
(cents/kilogram)	160.7	207.1	161.2
Percent change		28.9	-22.2
Iron Ore			
($/metric ton)	20.5	26.9	25.3
Percent change		31.2	-5.9
Bauxite			
($/metric ton)	34.3	41.2	37.0
Percent change		20.1	-10.2
Petroleum			
($/barrel)	12.7	28.7	33.4
Percent change		26.0	16.4

Source: Inter-American Development Bank.
Washington, D.C. (1985)

Latin America. In an effort to reduce inflation and
increase the profit rate, the U.S. adopted a policy of
reducing the money supply in the late 1970s. This policy
had the effect of increasing dramatically interest rates
and unemployment. As a result, imports in the developed
countries fell off and the world economy experienced a
recession in the 1980s.

Causes of the debt problems in the Third World,
particularly in Latin America, are not solely external.
Increased indebtedness among Third World countries
encouraged an expansion in the level of imports and
domestic expenditures. This development resulted in
substantial increases in trade imbalances in Third World
countries. Korner et al. (1986) place much of the blame
for the debt crisis on developing country governments.

> The debt crises are in most cases built into the
> economic, financial, and development policies of the
> governments of the developing countries . . . these
> classes prefer to indulge in luxury consumption
> rather than invest their money productively (p. 29).

IMPLICATIONS OF THE CRISIS

The international debt crisis has had two major
consequences for the United States. First, austerity
programs to improve the debt situation of developing
countries have led to further economic problems. The IMF
focused on imposing programs on the developing countries
that reduced inflation and purchasing power of local
consumers. The result has been a significant decline in
demand for goods produced in the United States.
Foweraker (1986) argues that the debt crisis has
contributed more to the trade deficit than have imports
from Japan. From 1981 to 1984, trade with Latin American
countries declined from a $7 billion surplus to a $16
billion deficit. The deficit with Japan increased by $18
billion during the same time period (Watkins, 1986). The
drop in U.S. exports to Latin America has accounted for
about one-fifth of the increase in the U.S. trade deficit
and about 800,000 lost jobs in 1985 (Foweraker, 1986).
The international debt crisis has also added to value of
dollar and slowed the rate of economic growth in the
United States.

The debt crisis, however, has significantly helped
one sector of the U.S. economy--finance capital. Kraft

(1984) argues that in the 1982 Mexican rescue, commercial banks benefited significantly from the deal.

> In assessing the deal two features emerge clearly. The Mexicans bought themselves a lot of time. While they paid roughly $150 million more in interest per year for eight years, they opened the possibility of negotiating the terms down later on. The banks, in return, received very juicy rates. They raised by half a point the average interest they were receiving on the rescheduled debt. They got for the new money a half point more in interest than they had received for the last big commercial loan to Mexico. The deal with Mexico set a precedent for similarly advantageous terms with Brazil, Argentina, and other countries (p. 5).

The debt crisis has also influenced American foreign policy. Cohen (1986) argues that it is difficult, if not impossible, for Washington to influence banks on foreign policy issues. The debt crisis has produced a growing tension between the banks, the state, and industry. The best example of this tension is the state's response to the debt crisis in Poland. When General Wojciech Jaruzelski declared martial law in 1981, the Reagan administration imposed several economic sanctions on Poland, with the intent of forcing Poland to restore Solidarity. These economic sanctions, however, also threatened to force Poland to default on its loans. When faced with a choice between maintaining its position against supporting the Polish government and supporting the interests of Western banks, the state chose to reschedule a portion of Poland's debt. The Polish case is an excellent example of how the U.S. state is constrained by capital flows, both nationally and internationally (Glasberg, 1987). Debt crises and capital flows have important social and political consequences that are frequently overlooked by economic analysts.

This relationship between state policy and international capital flows, however, was quite different for many of the Latin American countries during the present period. The large amount of debt has enhanced the influence of the U.S. state in foreign affairs in these countries. Because Latin American countries are interested in maintaining the flow of capital into the region, they are willing to let the U.S. state have greater influence during this period. Thus, increased indebtedness in developing countries does not automatically infer that these countries now have power.

Finally, the debt crisis has had an impact on the growth rate of Third World countries. The combined effects of monetary policies in developed countries and the IMF austerity programs in developing countries have reduced imports, inflation, and growth rates in Third World countries. Wage increases have been halted and government spending for the poor and underdeveloped sectors of the economy of Third World countries have stopped. Reduction in the growth rate of many Third World countries forced a restructuring of loans. Lombardi (1985) indicates that by 1982, four of every five dollars of new loans to the Third World were committed to repaying interest and principal on old loans. By 1984, almost all of the new loans were used to refinance existing debt.

One response by developing countries to the growing debt crisis could be to default on their loans. This issue was raised once again with Brazil's February 1987 decision to suspend interest payments to foreign lenders in February of 1987. Such a decision has important implications for the U.S. money-center banks. At the end of 1986, Manufacturers Hanover held $2.3 billion in loans to Brazil, which amounted to more than 61 percent of shareholders' equity in the bank. Bank America held over $2.7 billion in loans to Brazil, which represents more than 67 percent of the shareholders' equity. Citicorp, which holds $4.6 billion in Brazilian loans, more than any other U.S. bank, has reclassified these loans as nonperforming (New York Times, 1987a). This reclassification will cost Citicorp an estimated $190 million in earnings for 1987; its 1986 earnings were about $1 billion. Although regional banks in the U.S. have proportionally less invested in Brazil, many of the largest regionals would experience big losses if Brazil was to default. For example, Wells Fargo has $621 million in loans outstanding; Security Pacific has $585 million. These loans amount to over 20 percent of shareholders' equity in these banks. Other money-center banks and regional banks with loans to Brazil have followed the lead of Citicorp and have reclassified many of these loans. Although this step may reduce the profit rates of banks in the short-run, it should provide increased confidence in the banking industry in the long-run. These events, however, do suggest that the previous strategy of renegotiating loans may soon come to an end. A new solution to the problem has yet to be found.

One response by developing countries to the debt crisis might be to simply default on their loans, much in the same way that a company might declare bankruptcy. Macewan (1986) argues, however, that developing countries have three good reasons for not defaulting. First, it has been relatively easy for developing countries to reschedule debt. As long as banks continue to provide access to additional credit, their leverage in relation to the banks improves. Second, the austerity programs of the IMF serve the interests of the ruling class in those countries. Lower wages and reduced inflation permit the ruling class to improve their profits from local industry and provide them with additional capital to invest overseas. Finally, major defaults would probably would produce an international financial collapse, which would ultimately hurt even the developing nations. Although the developing countries recognize the perils of indebtedness, there are few viable alternatives available to them in the near future.

Thus, it would appear very unlikely that either banks or developing countries prefer to see the debt crisis end with any countries defaulting on their loans. A much more likely scenario that a variety of approaches will be employed to ensure the survival of the world financial system.

PROPOSED SOLUTIONS

Over the past five years, several plans have been proposed by creditors and borrowers to alleviate the Third World debt crisis. None of these plans has offered a long-term solution to the problem. Most of the plans consist of a variety of conventional ways of satisfying the debt, but fail to address the source of the problem--the inability of these countries to have enough dollars to meet interest payments over the next several years.

In addition to restructuring debt, a variety of novel plans have been proposed. One recent plan proposed by First Interstate Bank of Los Angeles involves a debt-for-commodity swap. According to this plan, First Interstate would export Peruvian asparagus, shrimp, and textiles and keep part of the proceeds as debt payment. The primary advantage of this plan is that it aids Peruvian exports.

The plan that has received the most attention in recent years is the debt-for-equity swap. Among countries involved in this plan are Mexico, Chile, and Brazil. In a debt-for-equity swap, a multinational corporation purchases at a discount part of a bank's Third World debt. The corporation turns around and presents the debt to the country's central bank for local currency, redeeming the debt at its face value. The plan has two key advantages. First, this plan encourages local investment. Second, the debt is erased without draining further the economy. However, some economists fear that debt-for-equity swaps will be inflationary. If central banks in debtor nations increase dramatically the money supply in these countries to redeem the debt, they would simply be replacing foreign debt with domestic borrowing. In addition, the debt-for-equity plans would promote increased foreign ownership of industry.

Although the debt-for-equity swap has been criticized by a number of progressive groups, a variation of this proposal has been implemented in Bolivia with some interesting results. Under an agreement between the Bolivian government and Conservation International, a nonprofit United States group, the Bolivian government has set aside 3.7 million acres of threatened tropical lowlands. In return for the protection of the tropical rainforests, Conservation International, a nonprofit United States group, has agreed to purchase $650,000 of Bolivia's $4 billion external debt. The $650,000 in debt was purchased for $100,000 (an 85 percent discount). Obviously, the U.S. banks were satisfied with the agreement because it retires some of the debt that many banks believe now will never be repaid. The Bolivian government was pleased with the swap, because there was very little cost to them.

The Bolivian plan represents a precedent and may encourage other countries to adopt similar plans to protect global resources threatened increasingly by the debt crisis. Growing indebtedness has encouraged Third World countries to bring additional marginal land into production as a means of repaying debt. As a result, the environment is threatened by austerity measures to increase exports in the countries with the largest debt problems.

The most publicized is the Baker Plan (named for the Secretary of the Treasury). This plan encourages major banks to make additional loans to Third World countries. In return, the debtor nations would agree to take

additional action to promote exports and reduce inflation
in their countries. The Baker Plan was first unveiled at
a joint meeting of the IMF and the World Bank in 1985.
The plan has two essential components (Pollin and Zepeda,
1987). First, U.S. banks would extend an additional $20
billion in new credit through 1988 and the World Bank
would lend an additional $9 billion. Second, to be
eligible for future loans, Third World countries must
make structural changes in their economies to promote
free trade and encourage foreign investments. This plan
was considered by many countries to be the most workable
until Brazil reported in 1987 that it could not pay the
interest on its loans. As a result, several banks, such
as Citicorp, decided to write off much of their Brazilian
loans, sounding the death knell for the Baker Plan.

One alternative for alleviating the debt problem is
simply to recognize that these loans will not be repaid
and adjust to these realities. Banks would accept their
losses.[3] This course of action means, however, that
economies of the developed countries would be forced to
accept bank failures and the Third World countries will
would adjust to having less access to external sources of
credit.

A popular alternative would stretch out debt payments
in a more orderly fashion. One mechanism for
accomplishing this would be for an agency to purchase the
troubled loans from the commercial banks and issue longer
term notes. This proposal, however, does not include any
suggestions for how this transfer of risk could be
accomplished. Finally, another proposal for alleviating
the world debt problem is to encourage international
coordination among regulators in the industrial countries
(Cohen, 1986). This plan would establish new capital
requirements for lenders participating in international
loans and limits on lending to Third World countries.
Again, one of the major weaknesses of this proposal is
that it does not specify how such an agreement could be
established politically.

Of course, one of the major obstacles to carrying out
a plan with long-term consequences is the power structure
in the world economy. Behind most of the austerity
programs imposed by the IMF and other agencies are
incentives for Third World countries to open their
economies to multinational capital. This solution is
imposed on developing countries, no matter what the
problem is. These programs are beneficial to the
developed countries because they encourage increased

production of raw commodities and increase the amount of exchange between developed and developing countries.

TRANSNATIONAL CAPITAL AND THE DEBT CRISIS

Debt crises are symptomatic of the contradictory nature of capitalist credit. On one hand, access to credit is critical for nation-states that are developing. Nation-states failing to gain access to credit, or paying higher prices for that credit than their competitors, will be at a disadvantage in the world market. On the other hand, dependency on credit has worsened the economic conditions in the Third World. Too much debt or the inefficient use of borrowed capital can increase dependency of Third World countries and promote increased inequality within these countries (Aronson, 1979). The debt crisis has contributed to the growing gap between advanced capitalist societies and the Third World. The debt crisis has enabled Developed countries to impose conditions on developing countries that open markets for corporations in the developed countries. Wood (1985) proposes that:

> the indebtedness that 3rd world countries incurred partly to avoid reliance on multinationals for domestic industrialization may prove, ironically,to be--in the era of debt crisis--the opening wedge for renewed and expanded penetration of the multinationals (p. 25).

The debt crisis has provided an important mechanism through which international capital is restructuring societies, economies, and states (DeWitt and Petras, 1979). Although it is probably too recent of a phenomenon to judge the long-term consequences, there is some evidence suggesting that the debt crisis has contributed to lower growth rates, increased inequality, and the feminization of poverty (Ward and Glasberg, 1986).

The rise of transnational capital exacerbates the contradictory character of capitalist credit. First, the mobility of capital is increased, which makes the problems of overspeculation even greater. National and international capital markets are becoming increasingly linked, which ultimately increases the volatility of capital. The result will be much more rapid shifts in capital flows and economic cycles.

Second, the rise of transnational capital encourages market solutions to debt crises. Market solutions favoring increased international trade as a means of repaying loans inevitably lead to crises in the world market.

> History has shown that the central bank of one country--even the powerful American Fed--cannot always by itself regulate currency movements in ways that will satisfy both bankers and industrial capitalists, much less satisfy workers and farmers. It seems that capitalism requires an international mechanism to regulate international currency markets and produce some semblance of stability. The major capitalist powers are now trying to recreate such a system, absent since the collapse of Bretton Woods. Even the free-market oriented Reagan administration has finally accepted this conclusion. But actually creating a working mechanism, in this period of capitalist stagnation and unsettled power relations among the leading capitalist countries, will be no easy achievement (Kotz, 1987:17).

Minsky's (1982) analysis of financial crises is useful for understanding the Third World debt crisis. Minsky argues that financial crises are a product of business-cycle expansion. With economic expansion there is a tendency for firms (or countries) to become increasingly dependent on external credit. In this analysis, I suggested that there were additional social and political factors contributing to the developing countries' growing dependency on external sources of credit. Minsky attributes most of the problems of financial crises to rising interest rates following the increased demand for credit during this period (Wolfson, 1986). My analysis suggests that increased interest rates, as well as lower profits and commodity prices, contributed to the debt crises. A major factor that Minsky ignores is the role of politics. The monetarist policies adopted in the United States contributed to many of the factors leading to the debt crisis. Indebtedness among developing countries also can provide additional political power to the developed countries and the ruling class in the developing countries. The debt crisis provides the ruling classes in many developing countries with a justification for policies increasing unemployment and reducing government expenditures.

Finally, Minsky (and other Keynesians) view the debt crisis as a liquidity crisis rather than a crisis of solvency in the Third World (Lombardi, 1985). This notion has important political implications. If the problem is viewed as a liquidity crisis, it is assumed that lower interest rates, higher growth rates in developing countries, and additional capital (primarily from public sources) will alleviate the crisis. If the problem is defined as a solvency crisis, structural changes in the Third World, and its relationship to the developed countries, are required.

Minsky may also place too much emphasis on institutional repairs as a means of addressing the instability produced by the financial system. The development of transnational capital and increased capital mobility make it increasingly difficult for an institution to influence the flow of capital.

NOTES

1. The exception is Bolivia, which suspended debt payments in 1985. It has not defaulted in the technical sense.

2. Wood (1985) contends that OPEC's role in the debt crisis should not be overemphasized. Euromarket expansion resulted, in most years, from non-OPEC deposits.

3. Most U.S. commercial banks have begun to accept the idea that they will have to take losses on Third World loans on a limited basis.

7

Credit, Policy, and Development

Credit is frequently considered a panacea for economic problems in lagging industries and regions, and less developed nations. Credit plays an important role in promoting economic development in advanced and developing societies. The rise of finance capital makes the allocation of credit an important determinant of growth and stagnation in sectors and regions. My analysis has suggested that credit tends to be allocated in an inefficient and inequitable manner for several reasons. Noncompetitive capital markets and government regulations may encourage lenders to direct capital in socially undesirable directions. I have suggested, however, that a more fundamental problem is the manner in which the credit system is structured to facilitate uneven development in capitalism. The conservative character of lending tends to favor borrowers with more assets and those considered less risky. In addition, the social organization of capital markets influences the performance of those markets.

Commercial banks are structured to encourage "safe and sound" lending. The primary source of funds for banks comes from deposits from the public. Maintaining public confidence in the safety and soundness of banks critically influences bank lending. As a result, commercial banks focus on lending that is basically low risk. The interest rate banks charge is relatively low, normally not exceeding a few percentage points above the prime rate. The inherent conservatism of bankers' operating procedures not to take risks produces a potential for the financial system to discourage entrepreneurial risk taking, particularly in a period of rapid technological change (Cox, 1986). This conservatism may lead to low corporate competitiveness and a technological obsolescence.

Another segment of finance capital, venture capital partnerships, is geared toward the opposite end of the market, high-risk, high-return loans. Venture capitalists provide equity financing to firms that will guarantee a 40 to 50 percent annualized rate of return. This high rate of return is necessary because after deducting losses and overhead, an annualized rate of return of 20 percent must be guaranteed to investors. Venture capitalists are, however, in a position to provide loans to a relatively small number of companies. The structure of commercial credit and venture capital partnerships produces a significant credit gap between the low-risk, low-return loans, and the high-risk, high-return financing of venture capitalists. This structure has important consequences for corporate competitiveness and development.

A frequent strategy for channeling capital to borrowers who fall into this credit gap is for the state either to provide loans directly to borrowers or to guarantee loans made by commercial banks. Under most circumstances, the state resists becoming involved directly in lending activities because of the potential competition to finance capital. Regulatory constraints often make it difficult for commercial banks to make low-risk loans even if guaranteed by the state. Alternative strategies must be developed to address these problems.

For these and other reasons, some sectors of capitalist economies may lack credit for development. It should follow logically that improved access to credit and lower interest rates will naturally produce development in those industries, regions, or nations that are lagging. My analysis suggests, however, that the relationship between credit and development is much more problematic than is often assumed. The three case studies show that _more_ credit may not be the solution to these problems. Credit is double-edged, producing some benefits, but also contributing to new structural problems in the economy. In a very real sense, credit is inherently neither good nor bad. The relative benefits of credit depend on the social and political context in which is allocated. To address these problems, we must not focus solely on the internal dynamics of capital markets, but we must consider how these markets are shaped, and in turn shape, social relations.

Access to cheap and plentiful credit in the 1970s

produced severe economic crises for U.S. farmers and ranchers and many developing countries. Borrowing to the "limit" was not only rational during this period, but also necessary, because of competitive pressures. The low cost of credit, caused by real interest rates' hovering around zero, encouraged capitalists to expand the scale of production. The rapid infusion of credit into a few sectors and countries led to overspeculation and eventually laid the basis for the credit crises of the 1980s.

In the case of regional development in the South, a shift in capital flows promoted the rise of the Sunbelt. The nature of this development was uneven, however, occurring primarily in the urban centers of the South (Rosenfeld, Bergman, and Rubin, 1985). The rapid flow of capital into many southern cities (e.g., Houston and Dallas) shifted to other regions as quickly as it moved into the South. Interstate banking and other aspects of financial deregulation threaten to undermine the financial basis of the region.

STATE POLICY AND CREDIT

Advanced capitalist societies have experienced economic stagnation since the mid-1970s. These economic problems have required the state to intervene increasingly into market economies. The credit system has been identified as a critical institution through which the state can direct industrial change. In the case of many European countries, such as West Germany, large banks play a very active role in promoting technological and structural changes in the economy. In Japan, there is an extremely close relationship between financial institutions and industry. This close relationship is frequently cited as an important factor in Japan's economic success (Brenner, 1986). In the United States, however, the separation between banking and commerce, the specialized nature of financial institutions, and the large number of banks makes it difficult for the state to direct capital flows and for financial institutions to play the same directive role as they do in these other countries.

From a policy standpoint, structural changes in financial markets strongly affect the state's capacity to influence market economies. Two contradictory developments in the United States will affect this relationship between state policy and credit. First, banking deregulation and centralization of the finance system should enhance the state's ability to influence the allocation of credit. In many ways, banking regulations established during the Depression are being circumvented by financial and nonfinancial firms. By encouraging the development of superbanks and a more centralized financial system the state is granting much more economic power to finance capital. This move should, however, improve the state's ability to negotiate with finance capitalists.

Conservatives and liberals appear to favor some of the recent changes in the financial system. Conservatives favor the expansion of market incentives in financial markets to create greater competition and less governmental regulation. Liberals favor a closer relationship between finance and industry to promote industrial change. Among the proponents of using the financial system to promote greater technological change and competition in industry are Robert Reich, Lester Thurow, and Felix Rhoytan.

However, development of transnational banks and the internationalization of the economy make it increasingly difficult for the state to influence domestic and international capital flows. The rise of international finance capital exacerbates the processes of uneven development. Internationalization of capital and increased capital mobility add volatility to capital markets. In addition, these developments put pressure on financial institutions to maximize short-run profits. Increased economic instability pushes the state to intervene increasingly into the economy to secure the conditions for accumulation. The state, however, is limited to treating the symptoms rather than the structural causes of the problem because of the nature of finance capital.

The capitalist state faces an interesting dilemma in its relationship to finance capital as it attempts to promote economic growth and development. If the state regulates the financial system as it has since the Depression to prevent economic crises, it is more difficult for the state to use the financial system to steer industrial change. Moreover, extensive regulations may encourage financial institutions to invest overseas. On the other hand, if the state deregulates financial institutions, capital flows may provide more constraints on state policy and could contribute to economic crises and instability. In a very real sense, the financial system has a dual character: it provides a mechanism for the state to direct economic change and is the cause of many economic problems and crises facing the capitalist state.

In addition to the options of taking a laissez-faire position toward capital markets or promoting increased intervention of finance capital into commerce, there are alternatives ways of structuring capital markets. Although most of these alternatives continue to be imbedded in capitalist social relations, they offer new strategies for channeling credit to underdeveloped industries, regions, and nations. These alternatives often involve a different social or political context for capital markets.

In the following section, I examine alternative institutional arrangements (public and private) for providing credit. These institutional arrangements focus on the issue of risk in capitalist credit systems and alternative methods of allocating capital.

ALTERNATIVES

Business and Industrial Development Corporations (BIDCOs)

One mechanism for directing capital to borrowers who have difficulty obtaining loans from commercial banks and venture capitalists is a Business and Industrial Development Corporation (BIDCO). BIDCO's use an approach referred to as a "risk return initiative." Developed in the 1970s, BIDCOs are structured to meet the financial needs of companies (particularly small businesses) that fall into the credit gap. BIDCOs have several methods of accomplishing this goal.

First, BIDCOs can make Small Business Association (SBA) loans and sell the guaranteed portion of these loans on the secondary market. By selling these loans, it is possible to leverage capital up to a ratio of 10 to 1. At the same time, BIDCOs are able to achieve an interest rate spread that provides them with a method of leveraging their own equity while maintaining a favorable return to investors.

Second, BIDCOs can borrow from private sources and make non-SBA loans. For example, a BIDCO can make subordinate loans with equity features. A BIDCO could make a 10 percent loan with warrants to purchase stock. The 10 percent loans make financing affordable to small businesses un able to afford financing. If the company is successful, it could mean as much as a 20 percent return on investments. Such a plan accomplishes several objectives: (1) it increases the accessibility of financing to small businesses while being sensitive to their cash flow problems; (2) it compensates the BIDCO for its risk and provides equity for more loans; and (3) it provides investors with a return comparable to that of venture capitalists.

A key advantage of BIDCO's and similar programs is that they can be directed to a specific sector, region, or group of individuals. This ensures that those in need will receive the most help.

Capital Access Programs

A second alternative to conventional financial institutions is a Capital Access Program (CAP). CAPs are based on much different principles from the traditional type of insurance or guarantee program. They are based on a portfolio or pooling concept. An example is the program developed by the Loan Loss Reserve Program of the Michigan Strategic Fund. Under this program, a special reserve is established for banks participating in the program to cover loan losses. The borrower makes a premium payment, and the bank matches the borrower's payment and the bank's payment. Borrowers and the bank must contribute between 1.5 and 3.5 percent. This means that the contribution to the reserve will be between 6 and 14 percent of the loan. The advantage of this program is that banks are partially protected against loan loss. If a bank makes a portfolio of loans under the program it will have approximately 10 percent of the total amount of its portfolio in the reserve fund. The full amount of the total reserve is available to cover any loan losses under the program. The purpose of the program is to make commercial banks more aggressive.

Capital access programs offer several advantages compared to other programs. The program is relatively nonbureaucratic, as banks can define the conditions under which they will make a loan. In addition, the program can leverage capital as much as 20 to 1. This means that the program would require a relatively small amount of public resources.

The program in Michigan has a number of restrictions on the eligibility of loans. For example, the Strategic Fund restricts loans to industrial, commercial, or agricultural enterprises within the state. The loan fund cannot be used for solely retail businesses, housing, or refinancing prior debt. Although the program is designed to help small businesses, there are no limitations on the size of loans. This program, however, would require some initial funding from the state.

Community Reinvestment Act (CRA)

Commercial banks are structured in a manner that encourages "safe and sound" lending, focusing primarily on low-risk, low-return businesses. Commercial banks can, however, increase their risk within these limits. In particular, many banks could, and should, provide more loans and services in black and low-income neighborhoods and communities and to small, especially minority, businesses.

Many community organizations have found the Community Reinvestment Act (CRA) of 1977 to be an effective tool for challenging commercial banks' lending practices and forcing them to be more concerned with local economic development. Congress passed the CRA and the Home Mortgage Disclosure Act to discourage lenders from "redlining" loans and services to neighborhoods on the basis of race or economic class of the population. More specifically, the act requires financial institutions to ". . . demonstrate that their deposit facilities serve the convenience and needs of the communities in which they are chartered to do business." Lenders are required to provide data on loans to the local community. Federal regulators review these data before a merger is approved and they are available for public scrutiny. Four regulatory agencies are responsible for ensuring that the credit needs of local communities are being met: the Board of Governors of the Federal Reserve System, the Comptroller of the currency, the Federal Home Loan Bank Board, and the FDIC. Because commercial banks are public institutions, they must demonstrate that they are contributing to the public good.

Community organizations and coalitions have challenged several bank mergers and obtained agreements with banks to provide an additional $3.7 billion for home mortgages, small businesses, and other loans to minority and low-income groups. These groups have found deregulation and the large number of recent bank mergers to be a foundation for local or statewide reinvestment campaigns.

The Association of Community Organizations for Reform Now (ACORN) has been particularly effective in negotiating with commercial banks to make more investments in local communities. In Phoenix, where interstate banking laws have resulted in the proposed acquisition of nine of the state's ten largest banks, ACORN has successfully negotiated a program for housing development. In St. Louis and New Orleans, ACORN won a series of negotiations with major local banks. These negotiations are important because they establish a baseline for other commercial banks in the region. More recently challenges have been made of major banks in Georgia and North Carolina.

CRA challenges have produced fifteen reinvestment agreements in the southeast. There are two different models under which these agreements have been negotiated (Carras, 1986). The first model involves a community organization's adopting an adversarial relationship with a commercial bank, particularly those banks in the process of acquiring other banks. An agreement is made that specifies future lending obligations to specific projects (e.g., housing projects and minority businesses). In this case, bank mergers present opportunities for communities to make more social demands on lending institutions.

A second model involves negotiation between a bank and a statewide organization (such as a legal services program) in a nonadversarial atmosphere. Usually these agreements do not specify the amounts to be reinvested in the community.

CRA challenges have taken place primarily in urban settings. There is some question as to how effective they will be in isolated rural areas, where it is much more difficult to develop an effective coalition among community organizations. In addition, the evidence suggests that regional banks tend to acquire rural banks that are relatively close to urban centers. If there is not a dramatic turnaround in the rural economy, regional banks are not likely to be interested in acquiring these smaller banks. Thus, community organizations in rural areas would have few opportunities to challenge the practices of commercial banks.

Social Investment Funds

Social investment funds have developed over the past decade in response to an increasing awareness that social change can be brought about through alternative investments. Social investment funds were established to ensure that investments will have a positive social and economic impact. These funds focus their investments on financing housing, the small business sector, educational loans, the Farm Credit System, and firms that contribute to the economic well-being of women and minorities.

Although the criteria for investments vary among the different funds, social investment funds tend to avoid investing in businesses that promote mergers and acquisitions, pollute the environment, produce weapons, or generate nuclear power. Many social investment funds will not invest in firms that discriminate in any manner against workers. The major goal of these funds is to allocate credit and make investments on the basis of social, rather than strictly economic, criteria. These firms seek to provide the highest return possible, while remaining consistent with the social and economic beliefs of their investors.

Among the largest social investment funds are Calvert Social Investment Fund, Working Assets Money Fund, Dreyfus Third Century Fund, New Alternatives Fund, Parnassus Fund, and Pax World Fund. At the end of 1985, these funds had assets totaling more than five billion dollars (Irwin, 1985). Most of these funds require a minimum investment, ranging from $250 to $5000. Socially responsible investing became an issue in the late 1960s when community organizations, consumer activists, and religious institutions began challenging the hiring practices, pollution standards, and safety regulations of many large corporations, such as Eastman Kodak and General Motors.

Harrington (1986:76) argues that a key to socially responsible investments is control of capital. "We feel that because we're in a capitalist system, the movement of capital is the most effective instrument to be used."

Social investment funds serve as an important alternative for depositors because they explicitly identify the social values underlying capital markets. Thus, social investment funds play an increasingly important ideologically role in uncovering the social nature of capital allocation decisions.

There are obviously many problems associated with
making socially responsible investments. One of the most
difficult problems facing these funds is deciding who is
worthy of their investment. For example, a corporation
may be considered excellent in terms of its environmental
practices, but have extremely poor relations with its
workers. One strategy for solving this dilemma, which
many of the investment funds have chosen, is to refuse to
invest in any corporation or activity failing to meet any
of their established criteria. This still presents
problems for socially conscious investors when weighing
the benefits and costs of these decisions. Recently a
major investment fund decided to stop investing in a
company that provided child care because the firm was
paying only minimum wages to its workers. This was a
difficult decision because such firms provide an
important service for working mothers. It is very
difficult to weight one social benefit against another.

CONCLUSIONS

Finance capital is a critical element in the economic
development and growth of industries, regions, and
nations. The relationship between the performance of
financial institutions and the nature and extent of
growth has received increased scrutiny in recent years.
Two factors prompted this concern. First, changes
occurred in the structure and performance of financial
institutions. Over the past five years, there have been
an unprecedented large number of bank acquisitions and
banks have expanded into activities unrelated to banking.
In addition, more banks have failed during this period
than any time since the Depression. Most of these
structural changes are related to the deregulation of the
banking industry that began in the early 1980s. Critics
of banking deregulation charge that these changes will
lead to a more highly centralized financial system and a
breakdown in the traditional boundary between banking and
commerce. These critics argue that deregulation will
introduce more instability into the economy and enhance
the power of finance capital.

On the other hand, advocates of deregulation contend
that these changes will make the financial system more
competitive, and therefore, efficient. These defenders
of banking deregulation contend that enhancing the
competitiveness of the financial system will improve U.S.

competitiveness in the world economy. In other words,
capital will flow to the most efficient sectors and
regions.

The second development spurring this interest in the
relationship between the structure and performance of
financial institutions is the poor economic performance
of various sectors of the U.S. economy, which has
contributed to uneven development and a trade imbalance.
Many analysts of the banking system point to the success
of other advanced capitalist societies (e.g., West
Germany and Japan) in which the financial system is
structured quite differently. In particular, the
financial systems in these countries much more
concentrated and are more closely linked to commerce than
is the case in the United States.

The poor performance of many sectors of the U.S.
economy is often attributed by neoclassical economists to
the relatively high wages of workers (because of
unionization) and too much government intervention (high
taxes and too many regulations). Following this logic,
the lack of competitiveness in these economic sectors is
not from lack of capital. Thus, neoclassical economists
argue that financial markets prevent capital from flowing
in an efficient manner. Banking deregulation will force
producers to adjust more rapidly to changing economic
conditions.

Keynesian economists take a much different position
toward banking deregulation. These economists contend
that banking regulations established in the 1930s were a
response to problems created by the commercial banking
industry. Deregulation will let banks once again create
instability in the economy. Keynesian economists tend to
agree with neoclassical economists that the financial
institutions are basically passive, simply responding to
demand. Keynesian economists argue, however, that
banking deregulation will lead to greater centralization
in the economy and make commercial banks less responsive
to demand. These economists would argue that the real
problem is that bankers are circumventing existing
regulations. As a result, a new set of regulations
should be established that maintain the stability in the
finance sector.

A third position further developed in this book, is
that financial institutions are not passive, but actively
influence the rate and extent of development. Financial
institutions, through their unique structural position in
the accumulation process, set parameters on the flow of

capital. Under most circumstances, control over capital flows is indirect. Theorists arguing from this third position see banking deregulation as exacerbating the tendencies of the financial system to contribute to uneven development. Centralization of the banking system and erosion of the boundary between banking and commerce more tightly integrate capital markets in the United States. This development should accelerate shifts in capital flows and introduce greater instability into the economy. A consequence of this development will be a greater emphasis on economic rather than social criteria in capital allocation decisions.

Centralization of capital markets promotes a much tighter relationship between the state and finance institutions, but does not necessarily improve the state's ability to control capital flows. Instead, the state is frequently more constrained by capital flows and is much more willing to negotiate with finance capitalists over policy. These developments have important policy implications. Increased integration of capital markets provides some advantages to policy makers because it potentially enhances the state's ability to channel capital into lagging sectors, regions, and nations. The increased influence of finance capitalists, however, tends to limit the ability of the state to address problems related to uneven development.

The structural tendencies of financial systems are exacerbated by the role finance capital plays in shaping corporate decision making. Much of the debate over corporate control has centered on the relationship of stockholders, managers, and banks to corporations. Increasingly, however, these debates have diminished in importance as more theoretical debates over the nature of corporate control (whether it is a direct process or a structural phenomenon) have become more important. Class cohesion and bank hegemony theorists adopt a structured view of corporate control; managerialists and bank control theorists conceptualize control as a direct process. The analyses of the farm financial crisis, the rise of the New South, and the Third World debt crisis suggest that banks may directly influence decision making and the flow of capital.

In the case of U.S. agriculture, evidence suggests that bankers increasingly influence decisions affecting farm operations. Although banks facilitated the rapid flow of capital into agriculture during the 1970s, this was primarily a response to state policy. The state has

increasingly reduced much of the risk in agriculture by
providing price supports, target prices, and crop
insurance. By reducing the risk in agriculture, state
policy indirectly encouraged capital investment (both
outside and within the industry). Thus, it appears that
agricultural policy was a key factor in the flow of
capital into agriculture. The farm financial crisis has
produced the potential for much greater influence by
financial institutions in agriculture. Through the large
number of farm foreclosures, financial institutions have
taken direct control over much more farmland. Whether
this signals a significant trend toward increased control
by financial institutions depends on the recovery in
agriculture and whether farmland prices rebound to their
previous level.

The rapid growth in the Sunbelt and the development
of the South's jumbo banks went hand in hand. This
growth, however, neglected many areas of the South; it
was largely urban development. In addition, this
development was based largely on low-skill, low-wage
employment. Banking deregulation makes this development
extremely precarious. First, continued investment in
low-skill employment is not very likely given the
competition form overseas producers.[1] Second, interstate
banking is permitting larger banks outside the region to
enter these markets. The result may be a net loss of
capital in the future.

In the case of the world debt crisis, the rapid flow
of capital into developing countries was a result of
banks's circumventing regulations in the U.S. and the
poor quality of investments in the country at the time.
The data suggest that financial control in developing
countries depends largely on the IMF to impose austerity
programs.

Recent changes in international and national capital
markets will only exacerbate the problems of development.
These problems can only be resolved by a radical
restructuring of the means by which credit is allocated
in capitalist societies. This restructuring requires a
demystification of the social and political nature of
capital markets. Capital markets, whether structured at
the local, national, or international level, are
constructed and influenced by human activity. From their
inception, capital markets are dependent on regulation
and security to attract depositors. Capital markets are
imbedded in social and political activities influencing
the direction and rate of capital flows. By denying this

social and political basis of capital markets, analysts
enhance the power of finance capitalists to direct
political and economic change.

NOTES

1. I am not suggesting that low-wage industries will
not continue to expand in the South. On the contrary,
there was substantial growth in these industries in 1987.
Much of this growth, however, was supported by Japanese
rather than U.S. banks.

Bibliography

Aldrich, Howard E. 1979. Organization and Environments.
    Englewood Cliffs, N.J.: Prentice Hall.
Aldrich, Howard E. and Jeffrey Pfeffer. 1976.
    "Environments of organizations." Pp. 79-105 in
    Annual Review of Sociology, Vol. 2, Alex Inkeles, ed.
    Palo Alto, Calif.: Annual Review.
Allen, Michael P. 1978. "Economic interest groups and
    the corporate elite structure." Social Science
    Quarterly 58:597-615.
Archer, Stephen H. and LeRoy G. Faeber. 1966. "Firm
    size and the cost of externally secured capital."
    Journal of Finance 21 (March):69-83.
Aronson, Jonathan. 1977. Money and Power. Beverly
    Hills, Calif.: Sage.
_____. 1979. Debt and the Less Developed Countries.
    Boulder, Colo.: Westview Press.
Bachrach, Peter and Morton Baratz. 1963. "Decisions and
    non-decisions." American Political Science Review
    57:632-42.
Balinsky, Alexander. 1970. Marx's Economics.
    Lexington, Mass.: D.C. Heath and Company.
Barry, Peter J. 1981. "Agricultural lending by
    commercial banks." Agricultural Finance Review 41
    (July):28-40.
Baumol, William J., Rensis Likert, Henry C. Wallich, and
John J. McGowan. 1970. A New Rationale for Corporate
    Social Policy. New York: Committee for Economic
    Development.
Bell, Daniel. 1958. "The power elite-reconsidered."
    American Journal of Sociology 64:238-50.
_____. 1961. The End of Ideology. New York: Collier.

Berle, Adolph, Jr. and Gardiner C. Means. 1932. The Modern Corporation and Private Property. New York: Macmillan.

Billings, Dwight. 1979. Planters and the Making of a "New South." Chapel Hill: University of North Carolina Press.

Block, Fred. 1977. "The ruling class does not rule: notes on the Marxist theory of the state." Socialist Revolution 7:6-28.

Bluestone, Barry and Bennett Harrison. 1980. Capital and Communities: The Causes and Consequences of Private Disinvestment. Washington, D.C.: Progressive Alliance.

_____. 1982. The Deindustrialization of America. New York: Basic Books.

Board of Governors of the Federal Reserve System. 1986. "The farm credit situation and the status of agricultural banks." Unpublished manuscript. Washington, D.C.: Federal Reserve System.

Brenner, Robert. 1986. "How America lost the edge: the roots of U.S. economic decline." Against the Current 1:19-28.

Brett, E. A. 1983. International Money and Capitalist Crisis. Boulder, Colo.: Westview Press.

Brewer, Anthony. 1984. A Guide to Marx's Capital. Cambridge: Cambridge University Press.

Brodeur, Paul. 1974. Expendable Americans. New York: Viking.

Bultena, Gordon, Paul Lasley, and Jack Geller. 1986. "The farm crisis: patterns and impacts of financial distress among Iowa farm families." Rural Sociology 57:436-48.

Burnham, James. 1941. The Managerial Revolution. New York: John Day.

Burns, Helen M. 1974. The American Banking Community and New Deal Banking Reforms, 1933-1935. Westport, Conn.: Greenwood Press.

Burt, Ronald S. 1983. Corporate Profits and Cooperation. New York: Academic Press.

Business Week. 1985. "The credit crisis isn't staying down on the farm." (30 September):90-91.

_____. 1986a. "Banking's balance of power is tilting toward the regionals." (7 April):56-64.

_____. 1986b. "Chemical finds out why they call it risk arbitrage." (26 May):40.

_____. 1987. "How 'Fast Eddie' is pulling First Union out ahead." (23 March): 142-43.

Carnoy, Martin. 1984. The State and Political Theory. Princeton: Princeton University Press.

Castells, Manuel. 1977. The Urban Question: A Marxist Approach. Cambridge, Mass.: MIT Press.

Center for Rural Affairs. 1986. "Redistributing the land." Center for Rural Affairs Newsletter (April):3-4.

Chayanov, A. V. 1966. "On the theory of non-capitalist economic systems." Pp. 1-28 in The Theory of Peasant Economy, Daniel Thorner, Basile Kerblay, and R. E. F. Smith, eds. Homewood, Ill.: Richard Irwin.

Cochrane, Willard W. 1979. The Development of American Agriculture. Minneapolis: The University of Minnesota Press.

Cohen, Benjamin. 1986. "International debt and linkage strategies: some foreign policy implications for the United States." Pp. 127-56 in The Politics of International Debt, Miles Kahler, ed. Ithaca: Cornell University Press.

Cox, Andrew. 1986. "The state, finance, and industry relationship in comparative perspective." Pp. 1-57 in State, Finance, and Industry, Andrew Cox, ed. New York: St. Martin's Press.

Dahrendorf, Ralf. 1959. Class and Class Conflict in Industrial Society. Stanford: Stanford University Press.

Davis, Kingsley and Wilbert Moore. 1945. "Some principles of stratification." American Sociological Review 10:242-49.

Davis, Lance E. 1963. "Capital immobilities and finance capitalism: a study of economic evolution in the United States." Explorations in Entrepreneurial History 1:88-105.

de Brunhoff, Suzanne. 1973. Marx on Money. New York: Unizen.

de Janvry, Alain. 1980. "Social differentiation in agriculture and the ideology of neopopulism." Pp. 155-168 in The Rural Sociology of the Advanced Societies: Critical Perspectives, Frederick Buttel and Howard Newby, eds. Montclair, N.J.: Allanheld Osmun.

DeWitt, R. Peter and James F. Petras. 1979. "Political economy of international debt: The dynamics of finance capital. Pp. 191-216 in Debt and the Less Developed Countries, Jonathan D. Aronson, ed. Boulder, Colo.: Westview Press.

Domhoff, G. William. 1983. Who Rules America Now?
    Englewood Cliffs, N.J.: Prentice-Hall.
Dreese, G. Richard. 1974. "Banks and regional economic
    development." Southern Economic Journal 40:647-56.
Eisenbeis, Robert A. and Alan S. McCall. 1972. "Some
    effects of affiliation among savings and commercial
    banks." Journal of Finance 27:865-77.
Elliot, John W. 1972. "Control size, growth and
    financial performance in the firm." Journal of
    Finance and Quantitative Analysis 7:1309-20.
Fitch, Robert and Mary Oppenheimer. 1970. "Who rules
    the corporations?" Socialist Revolution 1:73-107.
Foweraker, Joe. 1986. "Big banks and debt for all." In
    These Times 10 (39):5.
Fox, Kenneth. 1978. "Uneven regional development in the
    United States." The Review of Radical Political
    Economics 10:68-86.
Fraser, Donald R. and James W. Kolari. 1985. The Future
    of Small Banks in a Deregulated Environment.
    Cambridge, Mass.: Ballinger.
Friedland, William H., Amy E. Barton, and Robert J.
Thomas. 1981. Manufacturing Green Gold. Cambridge:
    Cambridge University Press.
Friedmann, Harriet. 1981. "The family farm in
    capitalism: outline of a theory of simple commodity
    production in agriculture." Paper presented at the
    annual meeting of the American Sociological
    Association, Toronto, Canada.
_____. 1980. "Household production and the national
    economy: concepts for the analysis of agrarian
    formation." Journal of Peasant Studies 7:158-184.
Gajewski, Gregory. 1986. "Rural bank failures not a big
    problem--so far." Rural Development Perspectives 2
    (June):2-8.
Genovese, Eugene D. 1965. The Political Economy of
    Slavery. New York: Vintage.
Gerschenkron, Alexander. 1962. Economic Backwardness in
    Historical Perspective: A Book of Essays.
    Cambridge, Mass.: The Belknap Press.
Gilbert, Jess. 1982. "Rural theory: the grounding of
    rural sociology." Rural Sociology 47:609-33.
Glasberg, Davita Silfen. 1981. "Corporate power and
    control: the case of Leasco Corporation versus
    Chemical Bank." Social Problems 29:104-16.
_____. 1985. "Finance capital and the social
    construction of corporate crisis." The Insurgent
    Sociologist 13:39-51.

_____. 1987. "Control of capital flows and class relations." Social Science Quarterly 68:51-69.

_____. 1987. "Chrysler corporation's struggle for bailout: the role of the state in finance capitalist society." Research in Political Sociology, Vol. 3 (forthcoming).

Glasberg, Davita Silfen and Michael Schwartz. 1983. "Ownership and control of corporations." Annual Review of Sociology 9:311-32.

Goldsmith, Raymond W. 1968. Financial Institutions. New York: Random House.

Goldsmith, Raymond W. and Rexford C. Parmelee. 1940. The Distribution of Ownership in the 200 Largest Nonfinancial Corporations. U.S. Temporary National Economic Committee, Monograph 29. Washington, D.C.: U.S. Government Printing Office.

Goss, Kevin F., Richard Rodefeld, and Frederick Buttel. 1980. "The political economy of class structure in U.S. agriculture: a theoretical outline." Pp. 83-132 in The Rural Sociology of the Advanced Societies: Critical Perspectives, Frederick Buttel and Howard Newby, eds. Montclair, N.J.: Allanheld.

Gramsci, Antonio. 1983. Prison Notebooks. Quinton Hoare and Geoffrey Nomel Smith, ed. New York: International Publishers.

Green, Gary P. 1984. "Credit and agriculture: some consequences of the centralization of the banking system." Rural Sociology 49:568-79.

_____. 1985. "Technocratic strategies of control: the case of the multi-bank holding company in rural areas." The Rural Sociologist 5:10-14.

_____. 1986a. "Capital flows in rural areas: an analysis of the impact of banking centralization on lending policies." Social Science Quarterly 67:365-78.

_____. 1986b. "Credit and rural development." Pp.415-21 in New Dimensions in Rural Policy: Building upon Our Heritage. Washington, D.C.: Joint Economic Committee, U.S. Congress.

Grubbs, Donald H. 1981. Cry from Cotton. Chapel Hill: University of North Carolina Press.

Gurley, J. G. and E. S. Shaw. 1955. "Financial aspects of economic development." American Economic Review 45:515-38.

Harrington, David H, Donn A. Reimund, Kenneth H. Baum, R. Neal Peterson. 1983. U.S. Farming in the Early 1980s: Production and Financial Structure. Economic Research Service, U.S. Department of Agriculture, Agricultural Economic Report no. 504.

Harrington, John. 1986. "Putting your money where your politics are: is the Left ready to do business? Socialist Review 91:65-80.

Harris, Laurence. 1976. "On Interest, credit, and capital." Economy and Society 5:145-77.

Harvey, David. 1973. Social Justice and the City. Baltimore: The Johns Hopkins University Press.

_____. 1982. The Limits to Capital. Chicago: The University of Chicago Press.

_____. 1985. The Urbanization of Capital. Baltimore: The Johns Hopkins University Press.

Herman, Edward S. 1973. "Do bankers control corporations?" Monthly Review 25:12-29.

_____. 1981. Corporate Control, Corporate Power. Cambridge: Cambridge University Press.

Hilferding, Rudolf. [1910] 1981. Finance Capital, reprint ed., Tom Bottomore, ed. London: Routledge & Kegan Paul.

Hirschman, Charles and Kim Blankenship. 1981. "The North-South earnings gap: changes during the 1960s and 1970s." American Journal of Sociology 87:380-403.

Hughes, Dean W., Stephen C. Gabriel, Peter J. Barry, and Michael D. Boehlje. 1986. Financing the Agricultural Sector: Future Challenges and Policy Alternatives. Boulder, Colo.: Westview Press.

Hussein, Athar. 1976. "Hilferding's Finance Capital." Bulletin of the Conference of Socialist Economists 1 (March):1-18.

Irwin, Robin J. 1985. "Clean and Green." Sierra (November):54-55.

James, David and Michael Soref. 1981. "Profit constraints on managerial autonomy: managerial theory and the unmaking of the corporation president." American Sociological Review 46:1-18.

James, John A. 1978. Money and Capital Markets in Postbellum America. Princeton: Princeton University Press.

Judis, John B. 1984. "Banking deregulation is key issue in economic debate." In These Times 8 (47):3.

Kamerschen, David R. 1968. "The Influence of Ownership
and Control on Profit Rate." American Economic
Review 58:432-47.

Kaufman, George G. and Roger C. Kormendi. 1986.
Deregulating Financial Services: Public Policy in
Flux. Cambridge, Mass.: Ballinger.

Kautsky, Karl. 1980. "Summary of selected parts of the
agrarian question." Edited by Jarius Banaji. Pp.
39-82 in The Rural Sociology of the Advanced
Societies: Critical Perspectives, Frederick Buttel
and Howard Newby, eds. Montclair, N.J.: Allanheld,
Osmun.

Kindleberger, Charles. 1978. Manias, Panics, and
Crashes. New York: Basic Books.

Korner, Peter, Gero Maass, Thomas Siebold, Rainer
Tetzlaff. 1986. The IMF and the Debt Crisis.
Atlantic Highlands, N.J.: Zed Books, Ltd.

Kotz, David M. 1978. Bank Control of Large Corporations
in the United States. Berkeley: University of
California Press.

_____. 1987. "The many causes of trade deficits." In
These Times 11 (16):17.

Kraft, Joseph. 1984. The Mexican Rescue. New York:
The Group of Thirty.

Lamb, W. Ralph. 1962. Group Banking: A Form of Banking
Concentration and Control in the United States. New
Brunswick, N.J.: Rutgers University Press.

Larner, Robert J. 1970. Management Control and the
Large Corporation. Cambridge, England: University
Press, Dunellen.

Lenin, V. I. 1917. Imperialism, the Highest State of
Capitalism. New York: International Publishers.

_____. 1938. Theory of the Agrarian Question. New
York: International Publishers.

Levine, S. 1972. "The sphere of influence." American
Sociological Review 37:14-27.

Lintner, J. 1966. "The financing of corporations." Pp.
166-201 in The Corporation in Modern Society, E.S.
Mason, ed. Cambridge, Mass.: Harvard University
Press.

Logan, John R. and Harvey L. Molotch. 1987. Urban
Fortunes. Berkeley: University of California Press.

Lomax, David F. 1986. The Developing Country Debt. New
York: St. Martin's Press.

Lombardi, Richard W. 1985. Debt Trap. New York:
Praeger.

140

Lundberg, Ferdinand. 1968. The Rich and the Superrich. New York: Lyle Stuart.

Luxemburg, Rosa. [1922] 1975. The Accumulation of Capital. London: Routledge & Kegan Paul.

Macewan, Arthur. 1986. "Latin America: why not default?" Monthly Review 38 (4):1-13.

Magdoff, Harry and Paul M. Sweezy. 1987. Stagnation and the Financial Explosion. New York: Monthly Review Press.

Mann, Susan. 1984. "Sharecropping in the cotton South: a case of uneven development in agriculture." Rural Sociology 49:412-29.

Mann, Susan and James M. Dickinson. 1978. "Obstacles to the development of a capitalist agriculture." Journal of Peasant Studies 5:466-81.

Mariolis, Peter. 1977. "Type of Corporation Size of Firms and Interlocking Directorates: A Reply to Levin." Social Science Quarterly 58:511-13.

_____. 1975. "Interlocking Directorates and Control of Corporations: The Theory of Bank Control." Social Science Quarterly 56:425-39.

Markusen, Ann. 1979. "Regionalism and the capitalist state: the case of the United States." Kapitalistate 7:39-62.

_____. 1980. "The political economy of rural development: the case of western U.S. boomtowns." Pp. 405-30 in The Rural Sociology of the Advanced Societies: Critical Perspectives, Frederick Buttel and Howard Newby, eds. Montclair, N.J.: Allanheld.

_____. 1985. Profit Cycles, Oligopoly, and Regional Development. Cambridge, Mass.: MIT Press.

Marx, Karl. [1894] 1981. Capital, Vol 3. New York: Vintage Books.

Masson, Robert T. 1971. "Executive Motivations, Earnings and Consequent Equity Performance." Journal of Political Economy 79:1278-92.

Meekhof, Ronald. 1984. Farm Credit Programs for Agriculture. Agriculture Information Bulletin No. 483. Washington, D.C.: Economic Research Service, U.S. Department of Agriculture.

Menshkov, S. 1969. Millionaires and Managers. Moscow: Progress Publishers.

Milkove, Daniel, Patrick J. Sullivan, and James J. Mikesell. 1986. "Deteriorating farm finances affect rural banks and communities." Rural Development Perspectives 2 (June):18-22.

Milkove, Daniel L. and David B. Weisblat. 1982. The Effects of the Competitive Structure of Financial Institutions on Rural Bank Performance and Economic Growth." ERS Staff Report No. AGES820226. Washington, D.C.: U.S. Department of Agriculture, Economic Research Service.

Mills, C. Wright. 1956. The Power Elite. New York: Oxford University Press.

Minsky, Hyman P. 1982. Can "It" Happen Again? New York: M. E. Sharpe.

Mintz, Beth and Michael Schwartz. 1985. The Power Structure of American Business. Chicago: University of Chicago Press.

_____. 1981. "The structure of intercorporate unity in American Business." Social Problems 29:87-103.

Mizruchi, Mark S. 1982. The American Corporate Network. Beverly Hills, Calif.: Sage.

Mooney, Patrick H. 1983. "Toward a class analysis of Midwestern agriculture." Rural Sociology 48:563-84.

_____. 1986. "The political economy of credit in American agriculture." Rural Sociology 51:449-70.

Munton, Richard. 1985. "Investment in British agriculture by financial institutions." Sociologia Ruralis 25:155-73.

Nader, Ralph. 1964. Unsafe at any Speed. New York: Grossman.

Nejezchleb, Lynn A. 1986. "Declining profitability at small commercial banks: a temporary development or a secular trend?" Banking and Economic Review (June):9- 21.

New York Times. 1986a. "As more family farms fail, hired managers take charge." (17 March):1.

_____. 1986b. "Bank deregulation crossroads." (3 May):3.

_____. 1986c. "Thrift ills disguised, study says." (18 August):25.

_____. 1986d. "World bank's farm loans." (19 May):26.

_____. 1987a. "Brazil's debt: a key juncture." (3 March):30.

_____. 1987b. "Citicorp may act on Brazil debt." (14 March):17.

_____. 1987c. "Foreclosed farms being sold as land values start to rise." (1 May):1.

_____. 1987d. "Many bankers upset by talk of superbanks." (10 June):29.

Nikolitch, Radoje. 1965. Adequate Family Farm:
    Mainstay of the Farm Economy. Washington, D.C.:
    United States Department of Agriculture, Economic
    Research Service no. 247.
Noyelle, Thierry J. and Thomas M. Stanback, Jr. 1984.
    The Economic Transformation of American Cities.
    Totowa, N.J.: Rowman & Allanheld.
O'Connor, James. 1972. "Question: Who Rules the
    Corporations? Answer: The Ruling Class." Socialist
    Review 7:117-50.
_____. 1973. The Fiscal Crisis of the State. New York:
    St. Martin's Press.
Office of Technology Assessment. 1986. Technology,
    Public Policy, and the Changing Structure of American
    Agriculture. OTA-F-285. Washington, D.C.:
    U.S.Government Printing Office.
Otto, Daniel. 1986. "An analysis of the farmers leaving
    agriculture for financial reasons: summary of survey
    results from 1984." Pp. 281-87 in New Dimensions in
    Rural Policy: Building Upon Our Heritage.
    Washington, D.C.: Joint Economic Committee, U.S.
    Congress.
Owens, John E. 1986. "The State Regulation and
    Deregulation of Financial Institutions in the United
    States." Pp. 172-230 in The State, Finance, and
    Industry, Andrew Cox, ed. New York: St. Martin's
    Press.
Parsons, Talcott. 1953. "A Revised Analytical Approach
    to the Theory of Social Stratification." Pp. 91-128
    in Class, Status, and Power, Reinhard Bendix and S.M.
    Lipset, eds. Glencoe, Ill.: Free Press.
Perlo, Victor. 1957. The Empire of High Finance. New
    York: International Publishers.
Persky, Joseph. 1973. "The South: a colony at home."
    Southern Exposure 1:15-22.
Piper, Thomas R. 1971. The Economics of Bank
    Acquisitions by Registered Bank Holding Companies.
    Federal Reserve Bank of Boston, Research Report no.
    48. Boston.
Piven, Frances Fox and Richard A. Cloward. 1971.
    Regulating the Poor. New York: Pantheon Books.
Pollin, Robert and Eduardo Zepeda. 1987. "Latin
    American debt: the choices ahead." Monthly Review
    38(9): 1-16.
Poulantzas, Nicos. 1974. Political Power and Social
    Classes. London: New Left Books.

Ranson, Roger and Richard Sutch. 1972. "Debt peonage in the cotton South after the Civil War." Journal of Economic History 32:643-67.

Ratcliff, Richard E. 1980. "Banks and corporate lending: an analysis of the capitalist class the lending behavior of banks." American Sociological Review 45:533-70.

Rosenfeld, Stuart A., Edward M. Bergman, and Sarah Rubin. 1985. After the Factories. Research Triangle Park, N.C.: Southern Growth Policies Board.

Sale, Kirpatrick. 1975. Power Shift. New York: Random House.

Sallach, David L. 1974. "Class Domination and Ideological Hegemony." Sociological Quarterly 15:38-50.

Saulsbury, Victor L. 1986. "Activities of U.S. banking abroad." Regulatory Review (October-November):1-13.

Schellhardt, Timothy D. 1983. "Interest Rate Gap on Business Loans Riles Small Concerns That Must Often Pay More." Wall Street Journal (13 October):31.

Schlesinger, Tom. 1987. "Crossing state lines: the South's jumbo banks." Southern Exposure 15 (2):33-36.

Scott, John. 1979. Corporations, Classes and Capitalism. London: Hutchinson.

Shepherd, William G. 1970. Market Power and Economic Welfare. New York: Random House.

Simon, Herbert. 1956. Models of Man. New York: Wiley.

Sinclair, Ward. 1987. "Getting a piece of the rock - and the farm." Washington Post (13 July) National Weekly Edition:21.

Skocpol, Theda. 1985. "Bringing the state back in: strategies of analysis in current research." Pp. 3-43 in Bringing the State Back In, Peter B. Evans, Dietrich Rueschemeyer, and Theda Skocpol, eds. Cambridge: Cambridge University Press.

Smith, Neil. 1984. Uneven Development: Nature, Capital, and the Production of Space. New York: Basil Blackwell.

Sorenson, Laurel. 1982. "Bankers agonize over dropping farm borrowers with access debt." Wall Street Journal (21 December):29.

Sorokin, Pitirim. 1953. "What is a Social Class?" Pp. 87-91 in Class, Status, and Power, Reinhard Bendix and S. M. Lipset, eds. Glencoe, Ill.: Free Press.

Sweezy, Paul M. 1942. The Theory of Capitalist Development. New York: Monthly Review Press.

144

Sylla, Richard. 1969. "Federal policy, banking market structure, and capital mobilization in the United States, 1863-1913." Journal of Economic History 24:657-86.

United States Department of Agriculture. 1985. The Financial Condition of Farms and Farm Lenders. Economic Research Service, Bulletin no. 490.

_____. 1986. Economic Indicators of the Farm Sector: Income and Balance Sheet Statistics. National Economics Division, Economic Research Service, ECIFS 2-2. Washington, D.C.

Verbrugge, James A. 1975. "Financing Rural Development." Paper presented to the Task Force on Southern Rural Development, Atlanta, Georgia.

Versluysen, Eugene. 1981. The Political Economy of International Finance. New York: St. Martin's Press.

Villarejo, Don. 1961. Stock Ownership and the Control of Corporations. Somerville, Mass.: New England Free Press.

Vogeler, Ingolf. 1981. The Myth of the Family Farm. Boulder, Colo.: Westview Press.

Ward, Kathryn and Davita Silfen Glasberg. 1986. "Foreign debt dependency and the economic status of women." Paper presented at the meeting of the Society for the Study of Social Problems." New York.

Watkins, Alfred J. 1986. Till Debt Do Us Part. Lanham, MD: University Press of America.

Watkins, Alfred J. and David C. Perry. 1977. "Regional change and the impact of uneven urban development." Pp. 19-54 in The Rise of the Sunbelt Cities, David C. Perry and Alfred J. Watkins, eds. Beverly Hills, Calif.: Sage.

Watkins, Thomas G. and Robert Craig West. 1982. "Bank holding companies: development and regulation." Economic Review 67 (June):3-13.

Weeks, John. 1981. Capital and Exploitation. Princeton, N.J.: Princeton University Press.

Wheeler, James O. and C. L. Brown. 1980. "The metropolitan corporate hierarchy in the U.S. South, 1960-1980." Economic Geography 61:66-78.

Wolfson, Martin. 1986. Financial Crises. Armonk, N.Y.: M. E. Sharpe.

Wood, Robert E. 1986. From Marshall Plan to Debt Crisis: Foreign Aid and Development Choices in the World Economy. Berkeley: University of California Press.

_____. 1985. "Making sense of the debt crisis: a primer for socialists." Socialist Review 15 (May-June): 7-33.

Wright, Erik O. 1978. Class, Crisis and the State. London: New Left Books.

Zeitlin, Maurice. 1974. "Corporate Ownership and Control: The Large Corporation and the Capitalist Class." American Journal of Sociology 79:1073-1119.

Zeitlin, Maurice and Sam Norich. 1979. "Corporate Control, Exploitation, and Profit Maximization in the Large Corporation: an empirical confrontation of managerialism and class theory." Research in Political Economy 2:33-62.

Zey-Ferrell, Mary and William Alex McIntosh. 1986. "Lending officer's decisions to recommend innovative agricultural technology." Rural Sociology 51:471-89.

_____. 1987. "Agricultural lending policies of commercial banks: consequences of bank dominance and dependency." Rural Sociology 52:187-207.

Zysman, John. 1983. Governments, Markets, and Growth. Ithaca: Cornell University Press.

Index